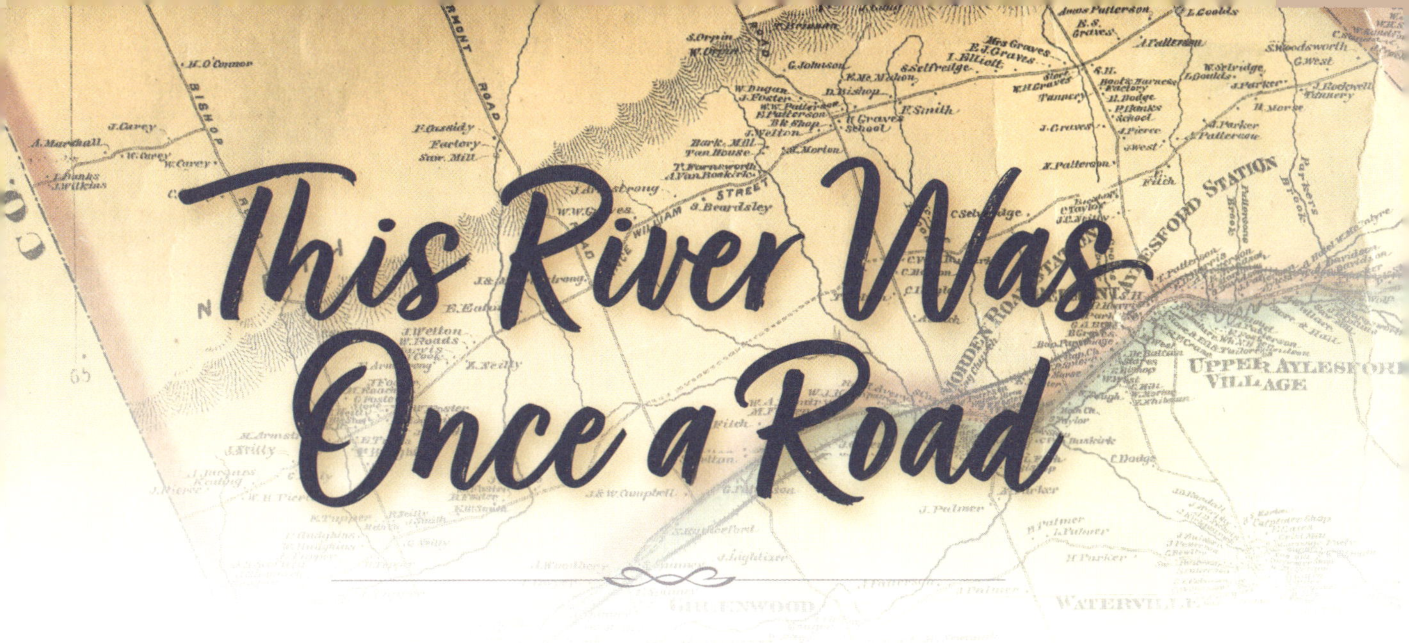

This River Was Once a Road

ABANDONED ROADS OF NOVA SCOTIA

Steve Skafte

I0445938

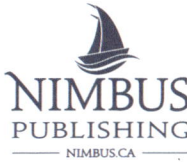

NIMBUS
PUBLISHING
NIMBUS.CA

Nimbus Publishing Limited

3660 Strawberry Hill Street, Halifax, NS, B3K 5A9

(902) 455-4286 nimbus.ca

Printed and bound in Canada

NB1768

Design: Jenn Embree

Editor: Raya P. Morrison

Nimbus Publishing is based in Kjipuktuk, Mi'kma'ki, the traditional territory of the Mi'kmaq People.

No part of this book may be used in the training of generative artificial intelligence technologies or systems.

Library and Archives Canada Cataloguing in Publication

Title: This river was once a road : abandoned roads of Nova Scotia / Steve Skafte.

Names: Skafte, Steve, author, photographer.

Identifiers: Canadiana (print) 20240508092 | Canadiana (ebook) 20240515684 | ISBN 9781774714270 (softcover) | ISBN 9781774714287 (EPUB)

Subjects: LCSH: Skafte, Steve—Travel—Nova Scotia. | LCSH: Rural roads—Nova Scotia—History. | LCSH: Rural roads—Nova Scotia—History—Pictorial works. | LCSH: Nova Scotia—Description and travel. | LCSH: Nova Scotia—History. | LCGFT: Illustrated works.

Classification: LCC FC2317.6 .S54 2025 | DDC 917.1604/5—dc23

DISCLAIMER

Every abandoned road in this book is listed in all current records as a public right-of-way. As such, all are open for anyone to use. The owner may be the county, municipality, Department of Public Works, or some other government entity—but public access is equally guaranteed, and cannot be restricted by any private individual.

Any detours off-road into surrounding properties may require permission. To be sure of sticking to the exact routes included in this book, please utilize the map on my website (see introduction).

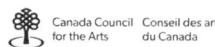

Nimbus Publishing acknowledges the financial support for its publishing activities from the Government of Canada, the Canada Council for the Arts, and from the Province of Nova Scotia. We are pleased to work in partnership with the Province of Nova Scotia to develop and promote our creative industries for the benefit of all Nova Scotians.

Contents

DARK SIDE OF THE SUN

walking
in the woods
I hear a chorus
of farmers afield in the forest
singing "Whistle While You Work"
you know the ghosts
of the good are porous
they let in the outsiders
patient rebels and time biders
you know the truth is of equal use
(out of the lungs of liars)
I put my faith in forest fires
destruction and desire
a bone we break so sorrow can set it
(burn it down before the clear-cutters get it)
and wasn't it good enough to keep going?
kill another kilometre
and the back of my mind
will make a good showing
and the tip of my tongue
dark side of the sun
love is the lightning
brought me home
to the thundering one
walking all that way
with the fear
I hear in the chorus
farmers afield
in the forest

Introduction

This book represents a decade of incessant adventures; ten years trawling through old maps and property records, searching for secrets the woods have kept from ordinary folks like me. I've found countless rock walls, old wells, rusty cars, vacant foundations, hunting cabins, and other signs of former human habitation. Each of these abandoned roads inhabits a time and place lost, a name on the map, a track through the wilderness that someone once called home.

I became obsessed from an early age, starting with the nearest tangled trail that scaled the mountain, rising from my Annapolis Valley community of Beaconsfield, twisting and turning up that steep switchback slope. Something about Chute Road held my heart tight. As I started exploring farther afield, first throughout Annapolis County, and later into Nova Scotia as a whole, I was amazed at the depths of adventure and the mysteries uncovered.

The effort is no small thing sometimes, and it's a journey where the end of the road is rarely the goal. The middle of nowhere is exactly what I'm after, a way to get beyond all the generations of clear-cuts and tangled young growth. It's a world of ankle-twisting, knee-turning, hip-grinding, face-scratching forgotten highways out here—one I think I'll never shake till I've left footprints on them all. Follow a few yourself, and I think you'll feel the same.

I'm a passionate believer in freely sharing my research with all those who might benefit, and as such, every abandoned road included in this book (and hundreds more besides) has been fully mapped out on my website: abandonedroadsNS.com.

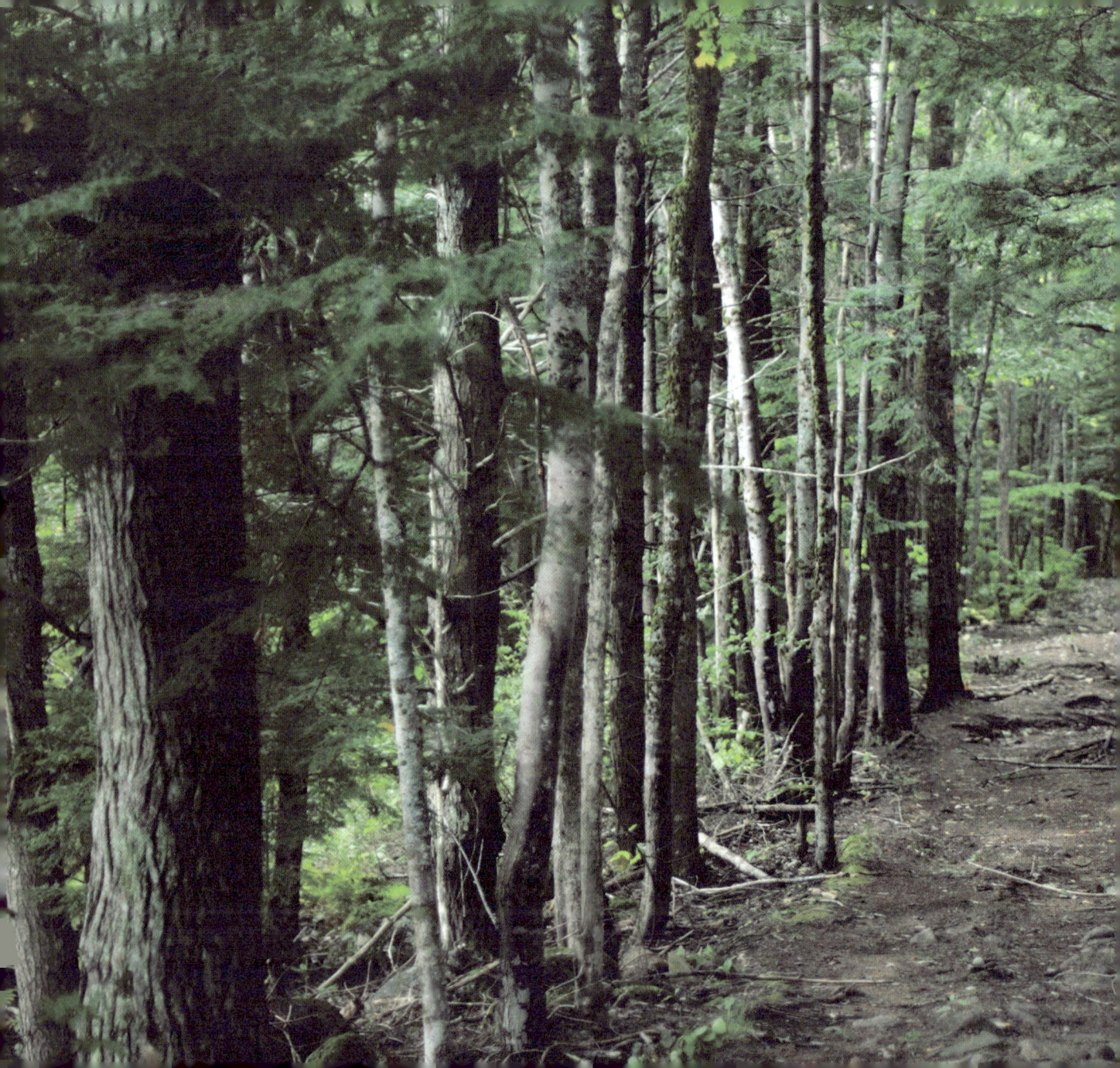

CHAPTER 1

Autumn Is a Long Way Down

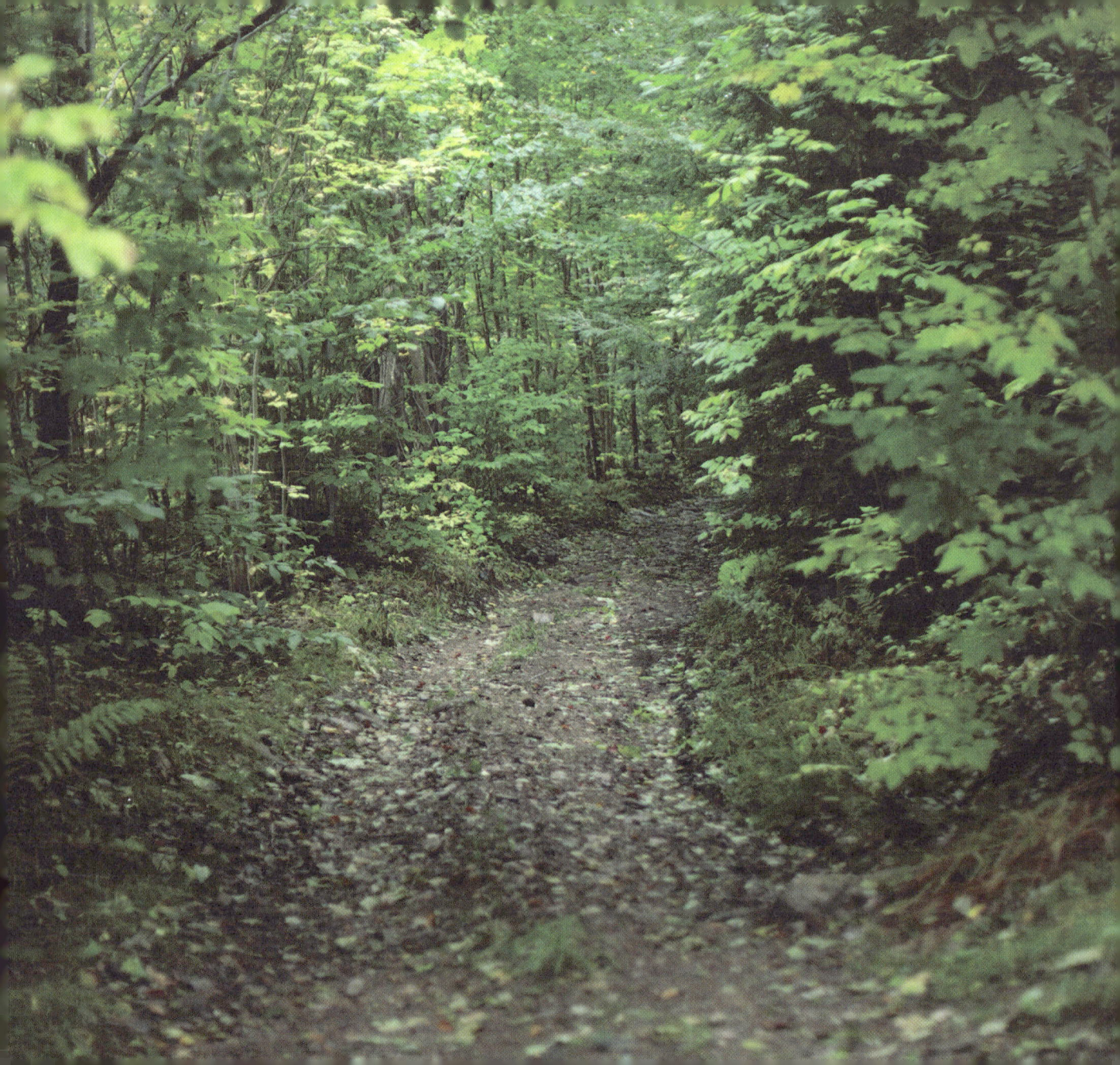

LITTLE BROWN ROAD

Rockland, Kings County

There's such a depth of sinking feeling when high ground goes low, you know it well when it's happened once. Now, I might say all sorts about open spaces, but close me in on a twisting road, and I'm sure to sing more praises. What can it be but comforting? Loose and loving are the ways it holds. Little Brown Road doesn't retain much width through the forest, just enough to let you through. Shepherd for the sheep that you've been, fuel for the feet you're dragging—walking all over yourself in your search for love. I find it not at the moment when someone says so, but exactly when and how heart recognizes heart. The tree that twisted the way my mind went, the emotional bend that upset my balance long ago. The fallen leaves of Hurricane Fiona underfoot, pulled from place like a reminder to be less belonging. This hike just might be talking me off the edge by bringing me to the lip of a better one.

There are few things I value more than these, the granite heads of my wild woods. I saw them for years as a nameless secret, artist unknown—until I finally met their maker, by the name of Brent Reeve. His carvings feel at once like comfort and menace, quiet pain and joy, only fully real when silent. Just like a crucifix might move someone deeper than any old art, I feel a similar measure for what lies here below. It's a spiritual experience gained in immediate abandonment. It can take the dereliction, weathered and hidden in ferns, swallowed by moss. These pupils will

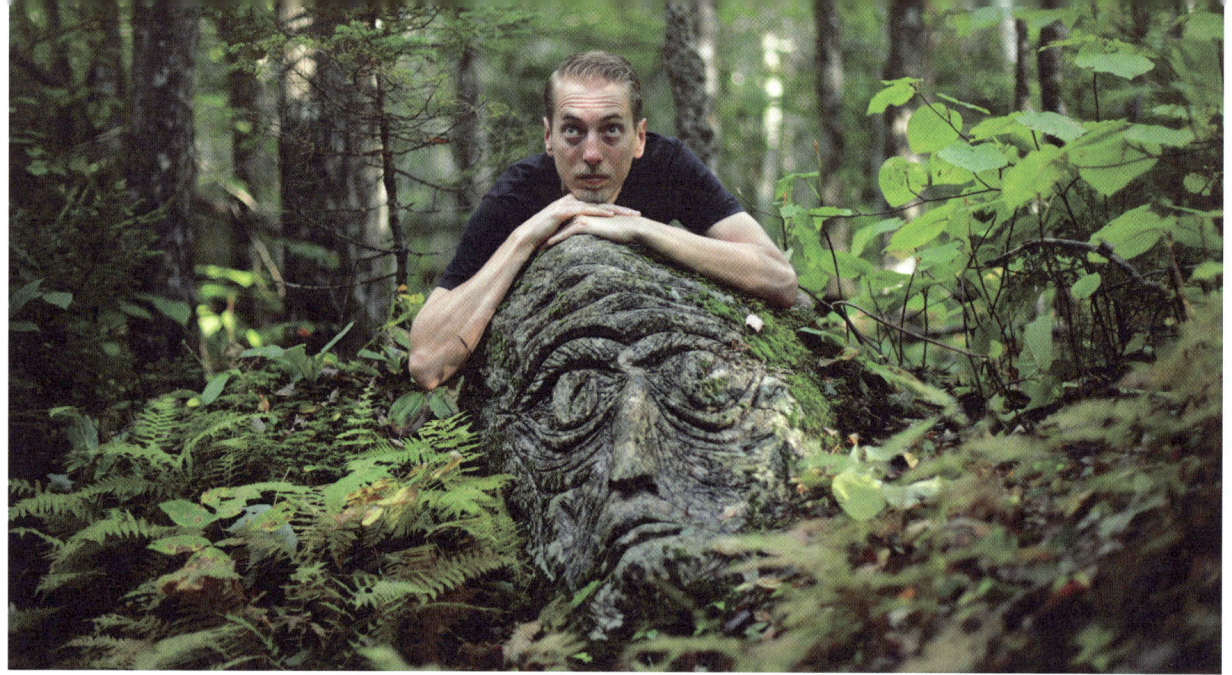

be watching for generations after mine have rotted, blinded forever in the face of all-seeing. In a century, strangers will be telling stories of what happened out of sight, wondering at the tales and meanings. Where lies the line between gods and characters, loved ones and graven images? All of me has eyes for all of you.

45.01257, -64.67561

2.1 kilometres. Runs east from the bend just after Civic #1564 on Prospect Road until maintenance resumes at Civic #430 Little Brown Road. Park on the shoulder at the corner.

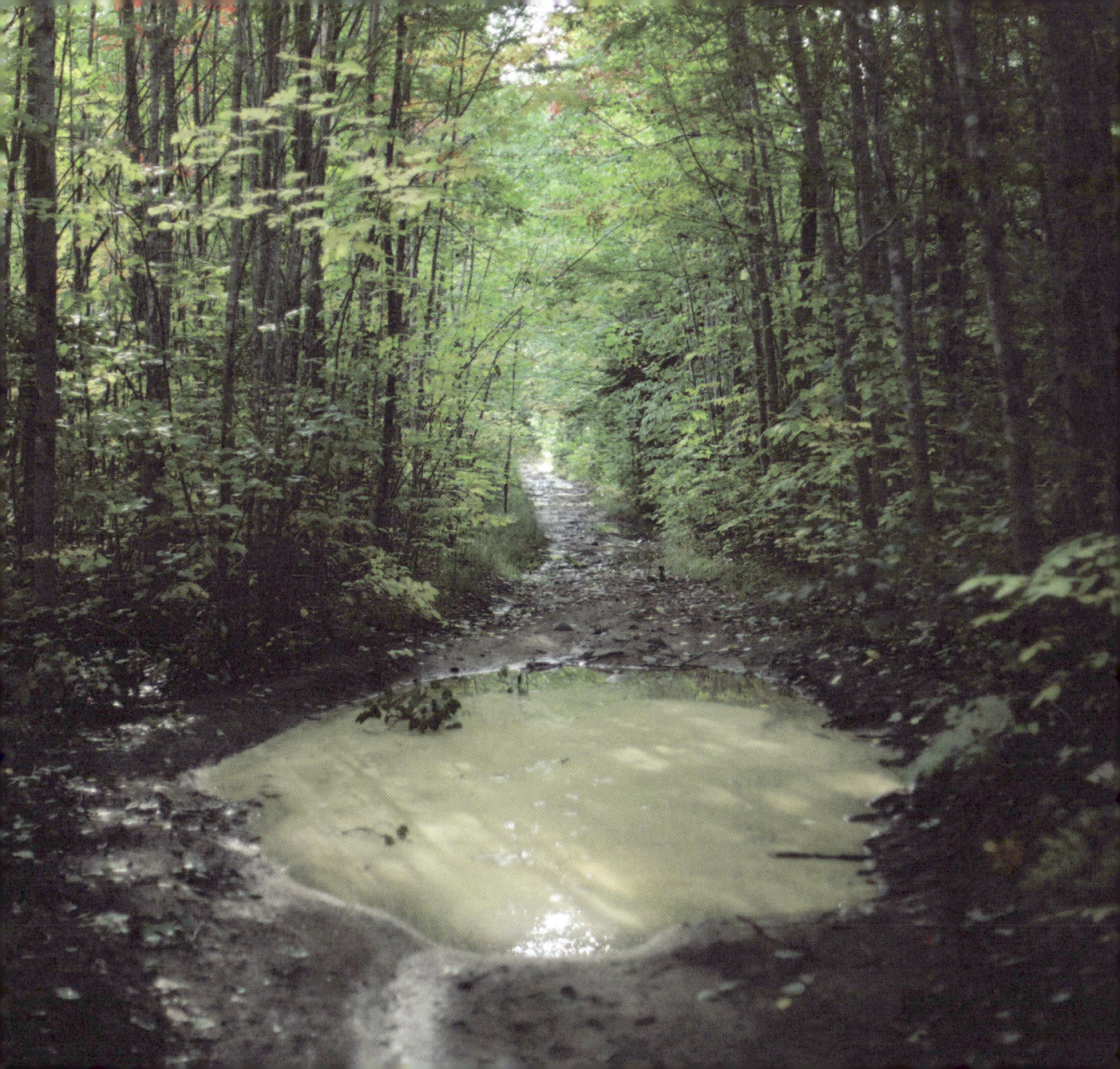

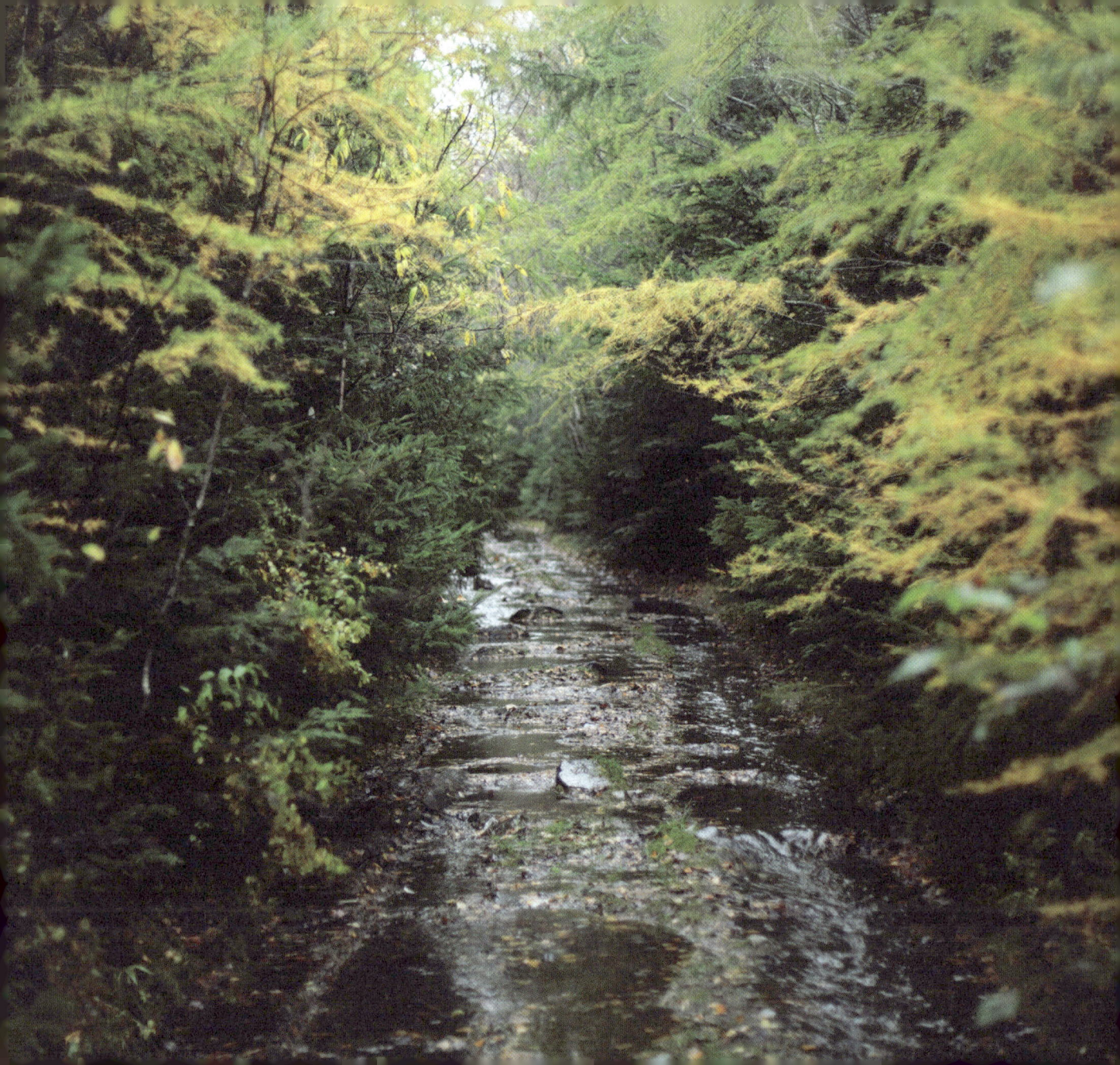

OSBORNE ROAD

New Canada, Lunenburg County

The washouts come down a corridor of larch, and this river was once a road, though you wouldn't know it now. Turning yellow all around; ankle-deep underfoot, I'm slipping in and going under with a daydream called the fall. Osborne Road is one straight shot along the river, a brief run of dereliction taken through the trees and left to linger. Gone low with what the downpour does, it'll be a while before the road runs dry again. You're better off not to walk this way with expectations; the wilderness has moods it can't control, and you can't love it less wild. Every effort to tame is harmful to both, so just be pleased with the space you've got for the journey. Last time I was here was in the sleepy afterwinter; now it's quickly coming back again. Won't be long before every branch is bare but the darkest pines, blending into black with the contrast of snow. It'll be shimmering sometimes, other days just dead and grey. For now, any storm is worth the chaos, chasing down the colour soon to slip, so to speak. On days like these, I'm easily reminded—I do my best dreaming wide awake.

Wynock and Mossman families once settled here, their tales all washed away. A tiny trickle turned wild is the soul of autumn lingering, bursting banks in search of a brook with wider shoulders. These streams have no names, but they're in a rush to join the LaHave River down below, chasing autumn leaves

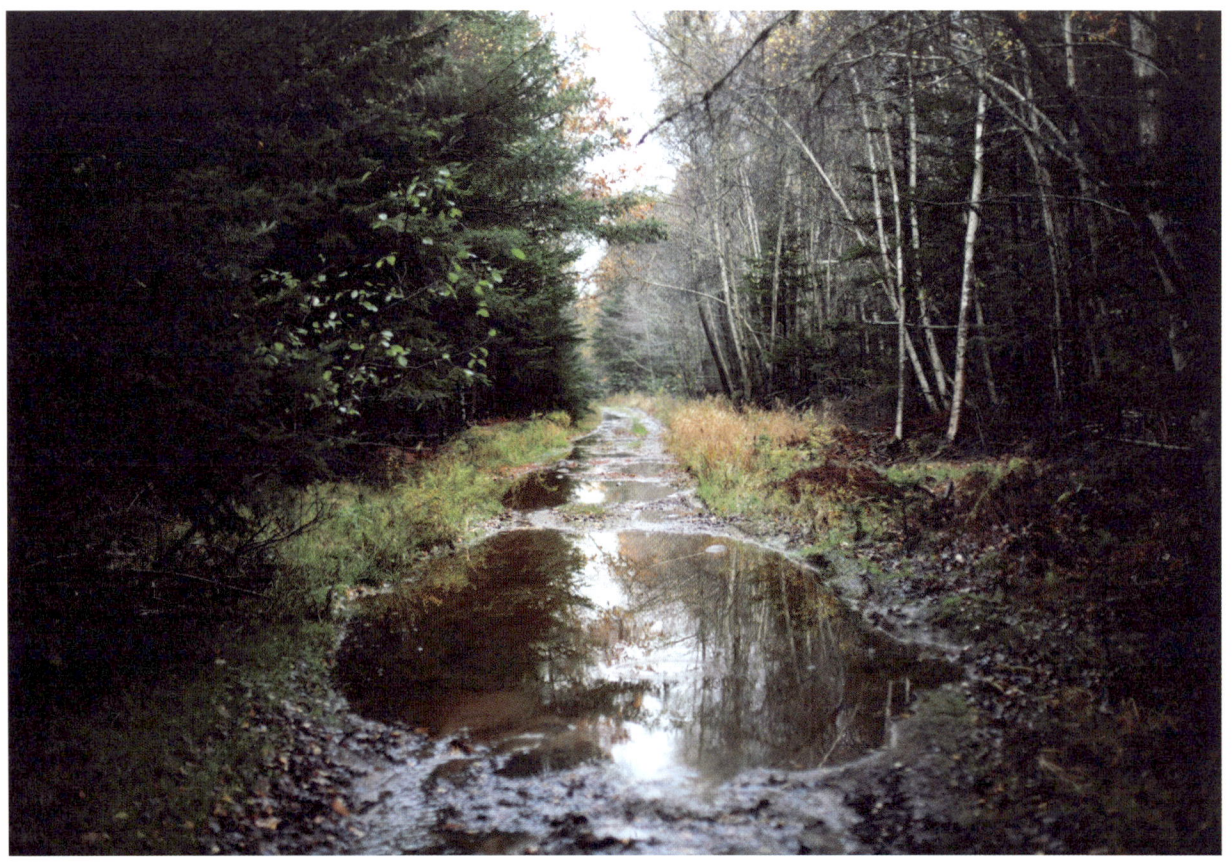

and fallen needles in its wake. Bending to the east until west calls back again, centuries of least resistance slowly shaping a path to take. You could cross wherever you like, one wide leap would make it, if you find yourself locked on the wrong land. You could demand an escape, a fiery-eyed freedom taken step by weightless step. It's the adrenaline running rampant that washes off your aches and pains, trains your heart

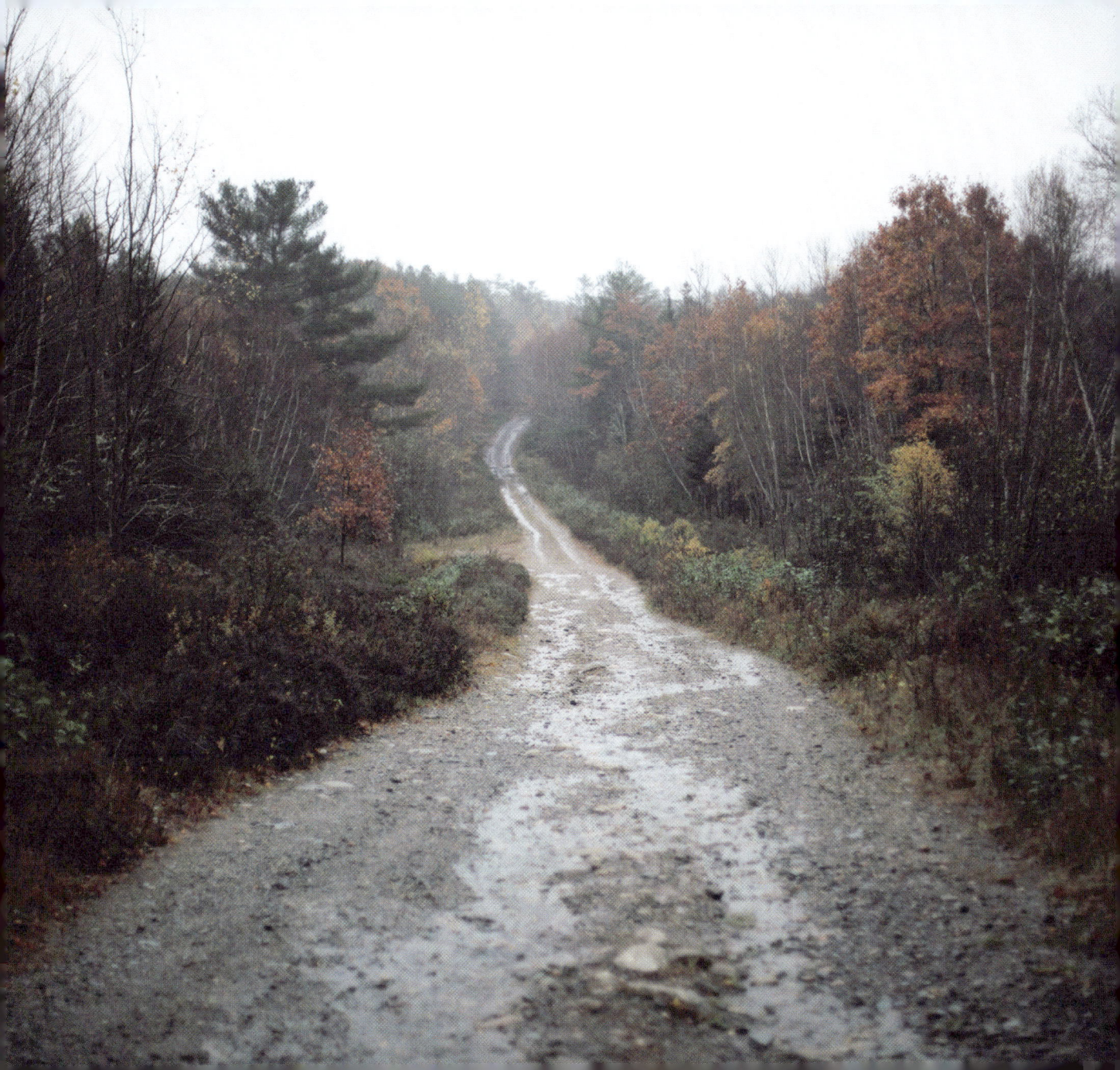

to feel alive again. Chasing tiny rapids and a restless rustling, blood thumping, splashing brighter colours to the canvas called my eyes. Get a good reason to blink, trap the world behind your lids and remember. That's what I say every morning after waking—don't go to bed again unless you've been breathless at least once.

44.51632, -64.68405

2.5 kilometres. Runs southeast along the LaHave River from Civic #673 to #135. Park at the wide spot where the pavement ends.

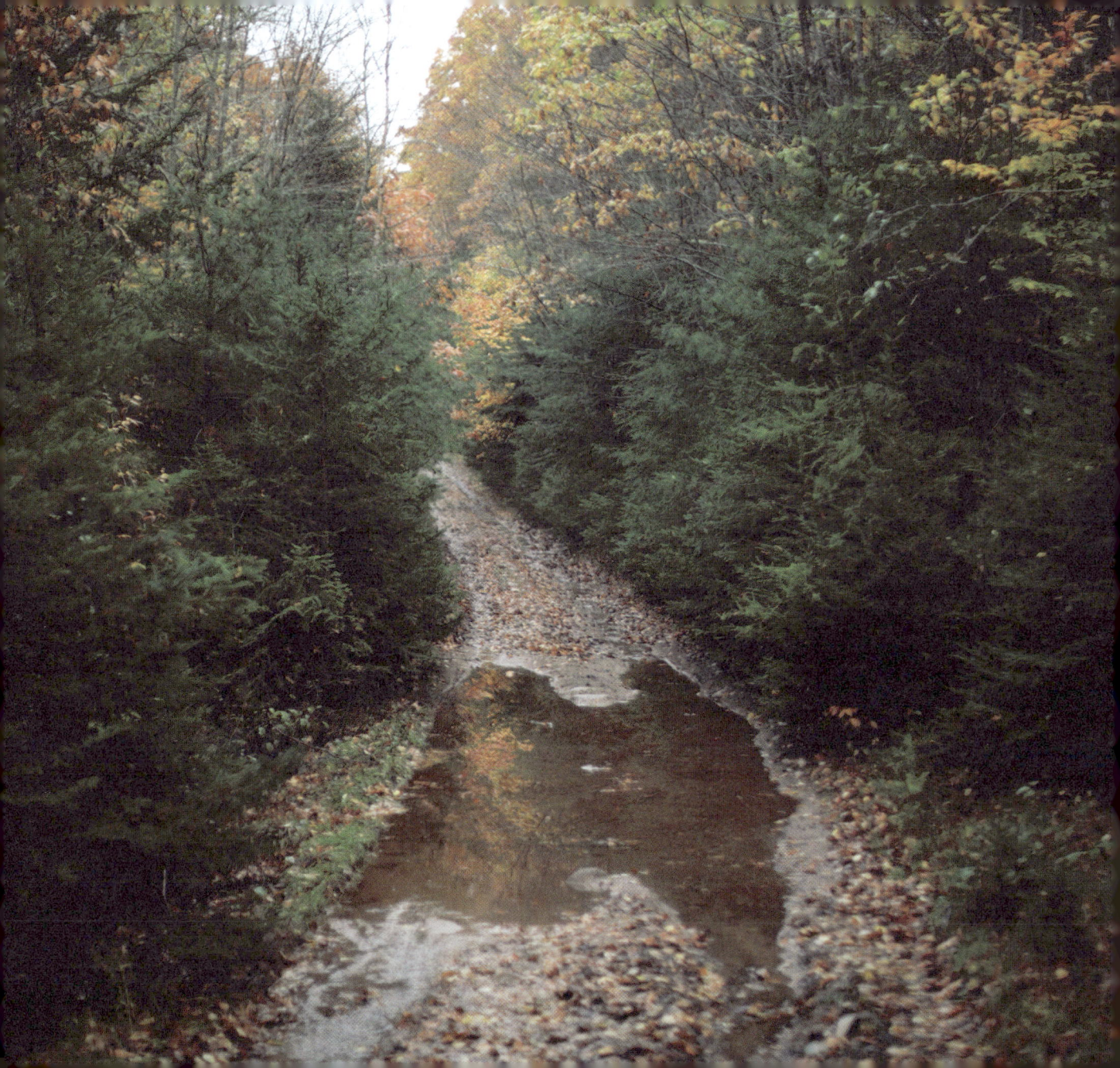

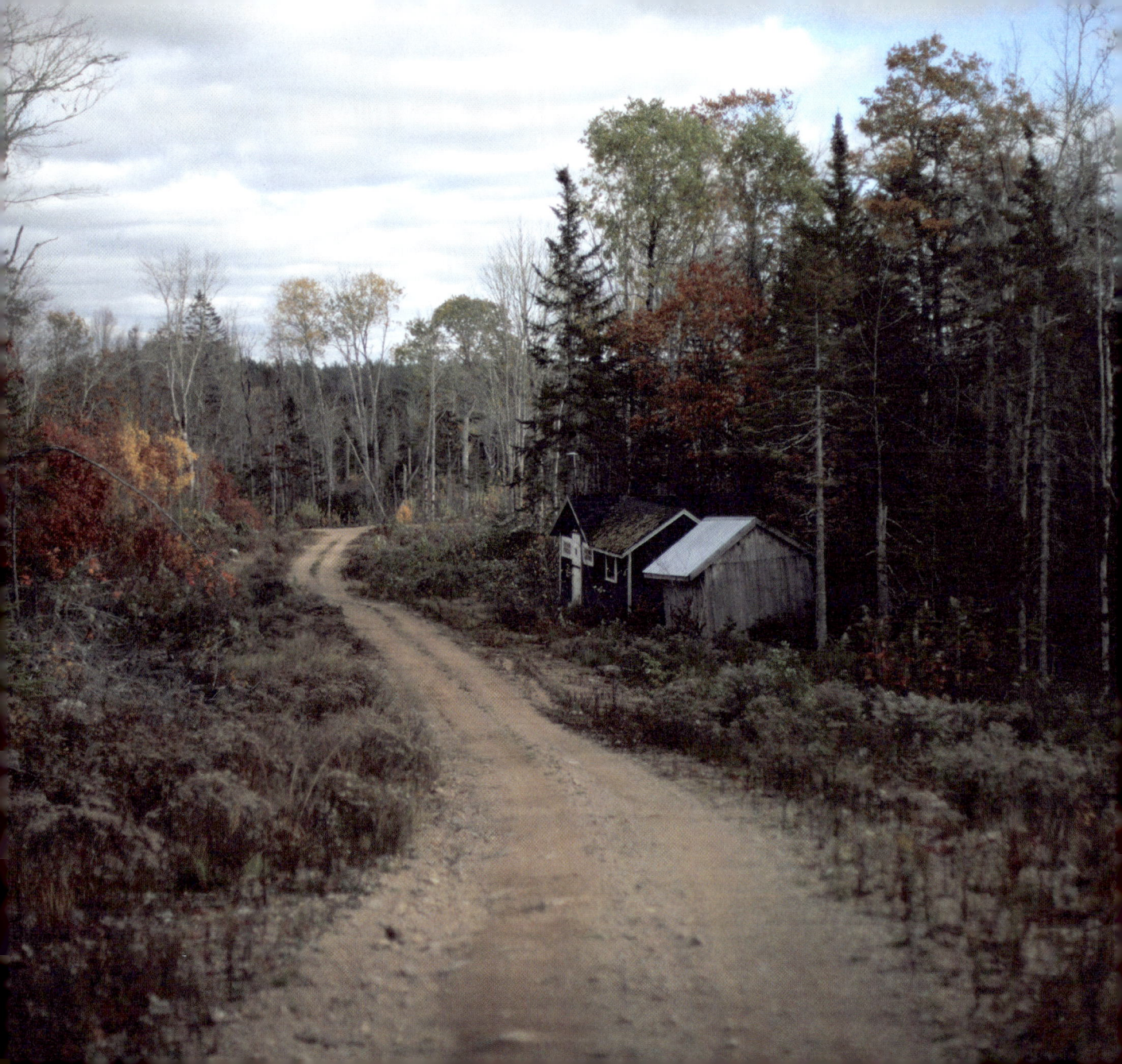

OLD DALHOUSIE ROAD

Springfield, Annapolis County

When you start out down the Old Dalhousie Road, it's hard believing how this was once the main way through these woods. Now it's just a trail between the east and west communities, sometimes logged, sometimes not, carrying on to an eventual dead end. All the way is a little adventure—first through the forest off Highway 10, across the old Nova Scotia Central Railway bed and past some cabins, into a windswept clear-cut, then over the Upper Thirty Lake bridge. Then it's up into the woods again a while before breaking to a second clear-cut that lasts a little too long. Finally, it's wooded again for the last of the journey, falling down to where the LaHave River bridge once stood. Long washed out now,

only the granite abutments remaining; no manner of a span to cross it. These abandoned roads are the opposite of shortcuts because, even when they take a straighter tack, terrain conspires to drive you slower than the wide way around. The chill was real this Sunday afternoon, "mix of sun and cloud," to quote the weatherman. It was cold for the first time after a warm and wistful autumn, slow intrusion to the body heat; I was warm by maybe halfway through the hike. These are the best times to go stumbling through the forest: no snow and ice, no insects, still plenty of spreading shade. The derelict past holds a better share of mystery before winter comes to trade it all for starkness. I've got all the wonder I could want here.

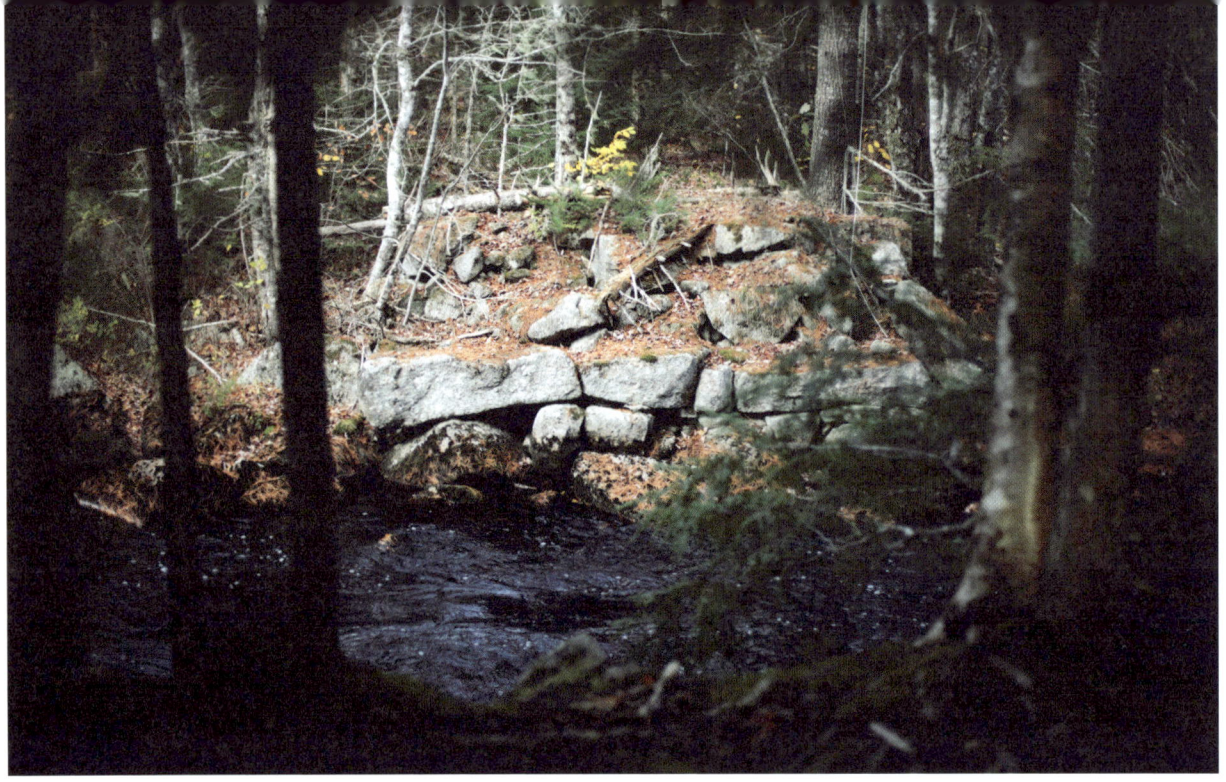

Like a steady musical rhythm building to a beat, many abandoned roads have a drop to them. It's hard to describe, like the bottom falls out, but you just don't mind it, things coming to a stop prematurely. You can't take Old Dalhousie Road all the way anywhere anymore, but into your own mind and imagination—absolutely. I feel blinded when it's all too open, maybe a little menaced when it's growing shoulder to shoulder. But whatever the mood that's been chasing me on the way, I think I believe I'm belonging. Not in that "back to the land" kind of way, like I want to build a cabin here and only rarely escape for supplies. No, it's more like that feeling of being with someone you love, like long talks with my wife when I remember I'm human. It's right, but wouldn't be if there was no space to breathe in. Between people, there's always off-and-on

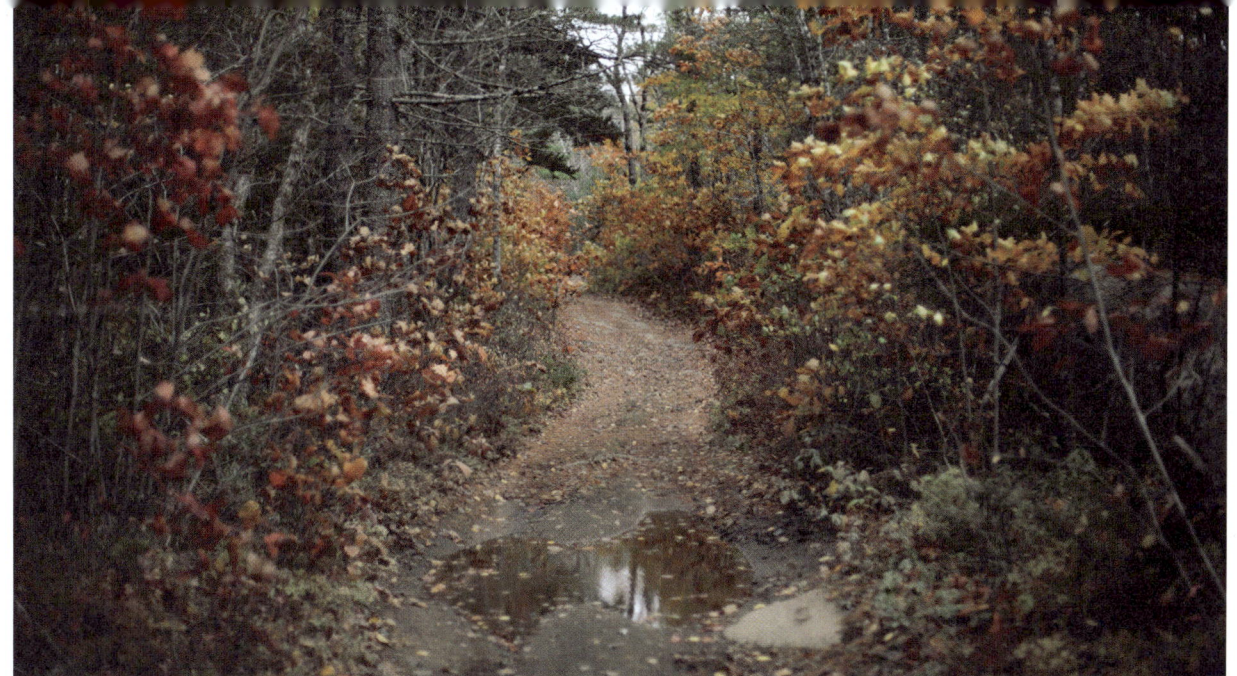

aloneness, time off in work or necessary distance. I feel the same for the forest. A deep and abiding love, but a desire to take and leave it. I'll always be back, with the same kind of passion as last time.

44.70495, -64.94087

5.9 kilometres. Runs east from Highway 10 to the site of a former bridge across the LaHave River. Park at the wide spot on the highway shoulder.

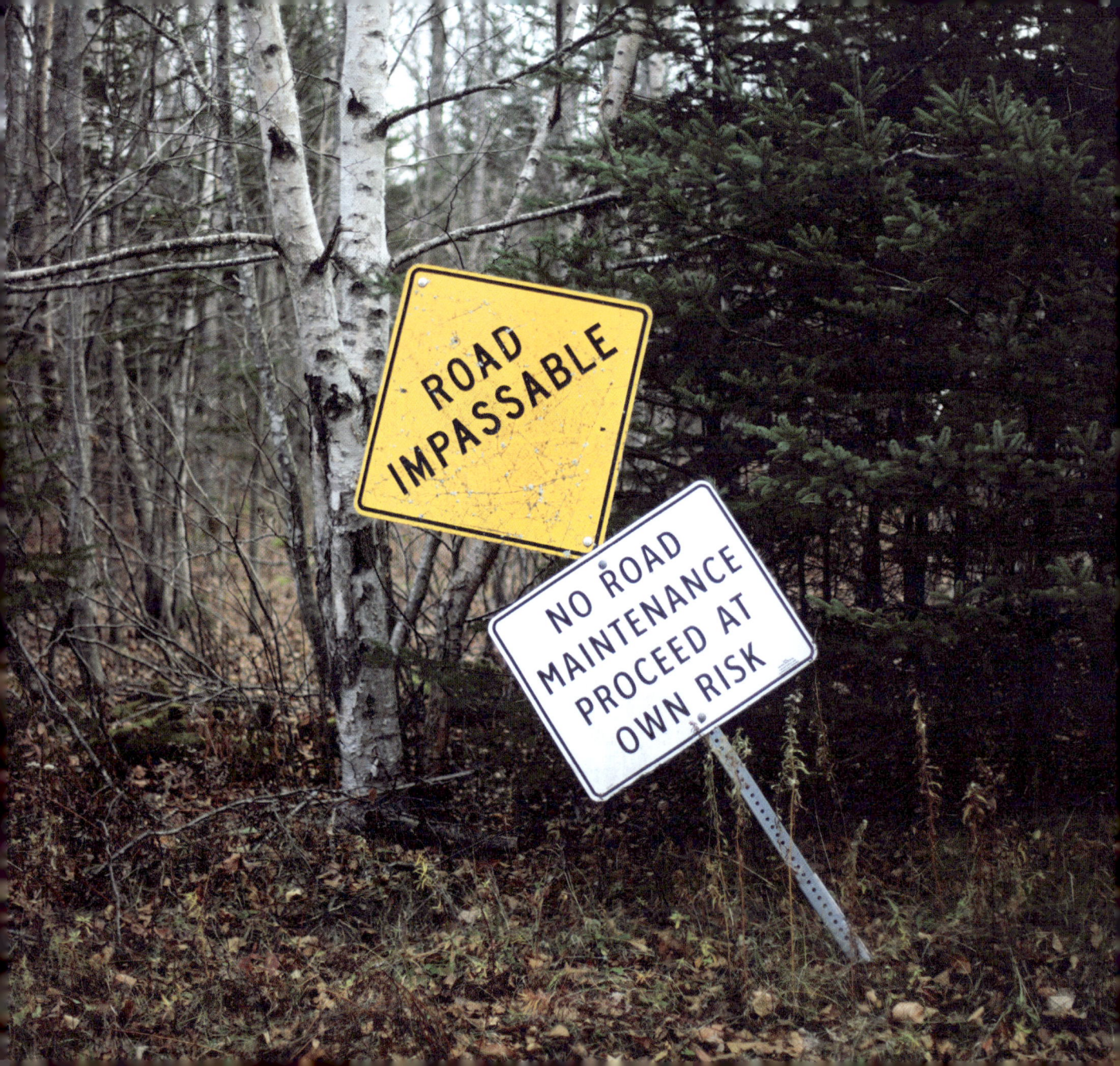

AUSTRALIA ROAD

Morden, Kings County

Usually unmarked, abandoned roads are periodically posted with my version of a welcome sign. Proceed at own risk? Sure thing, finally something I can call my own. Australia Road comes with an addition, one I've never seen elsewhere. Road Impassable is a true warning for any old road car, but it doesn't ring right if you're pushing through on foot. Probably posted when the bridge first washed out, halfway between here and Victoria Road. Now it's home to a wide, rusty culvert, enough to keep you on your way. It was an unusually busy day in this bit of the woods, as I passed two trucks and a gaggle of redneck off-roaders. Good old boys rolling, shouting greetings over engines sputtering. I spotted an old

Holiday-brand trailer, shot through a thousand times for target practice. I walked into the edge of autumn evening and made it out with gloaming chasing.

I take every chance I get to climb down into an old foundation and clear away the brush. Dry stacked stones are a subtle sight, one that blends into obscurity quickly, and it's tough to get a good look with everything wild in the way. This one took about an hour to open up, cutting a mix of young shoots and rotted trunks. There's a lot of competition for light down there, in the long-exposed cellars that were dug to live in darkness. In the early days, the woods just west of Robinson Brook were populated by the Husey family — so these crumbling walls were likely

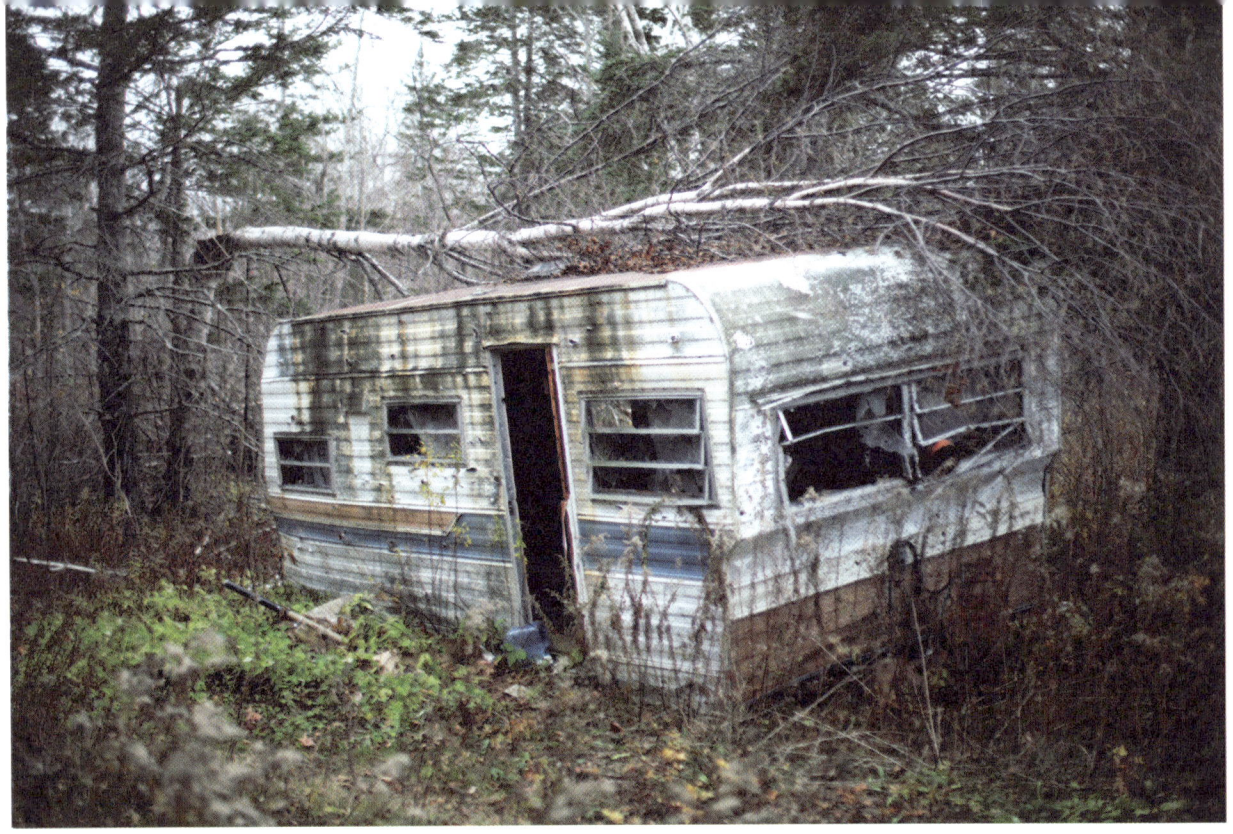

raised by them. There were Blew and Stark houses farther east, as well. They helped make up the long-gone community of Australia, said to be named by a man who wanted to visit that country, but never did. It was all eventually abandoned, the area absorbed into nearby Morden, with only muddy ruts left to carry the name. They run just out of sight of the homestead, where creaking centuries-old trees in the distance mark a faded driveway. Two massive trunks that were planted by the original settlers, they've both outlived their progenitors by a century.

The wilderness is overwhelmingly crowded with tracks and trails, of course, twisting and turning—but only a select few of them have a name. Those are

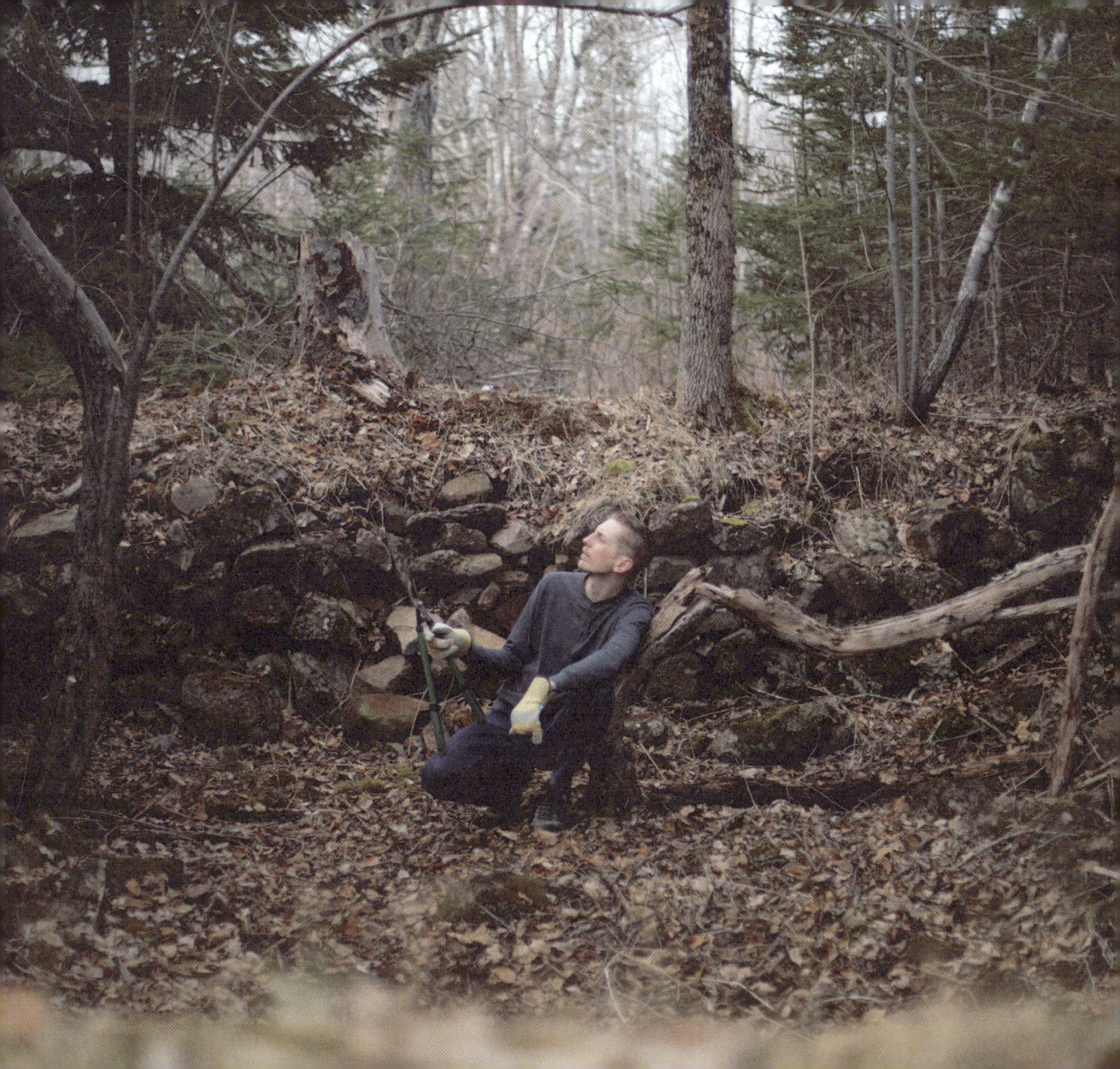

the ones that draw me out, as real to me as people I've known, waiting on their story to be filled by written records, oral history, assumptions or guesses. Whatever gets you going down abandoned roads, kicking through on the way to making sure that nature doesn't borrow them back. I've discovered that they help me feel a little more at home. Who's to say you don't belong in a world where no one does?

45.07906, -64.91324

3.7 kilometres. Runs east from Civic #29 (the only house) through the Robinson Brook hollow to Victoria Road. Park on the shoulder.

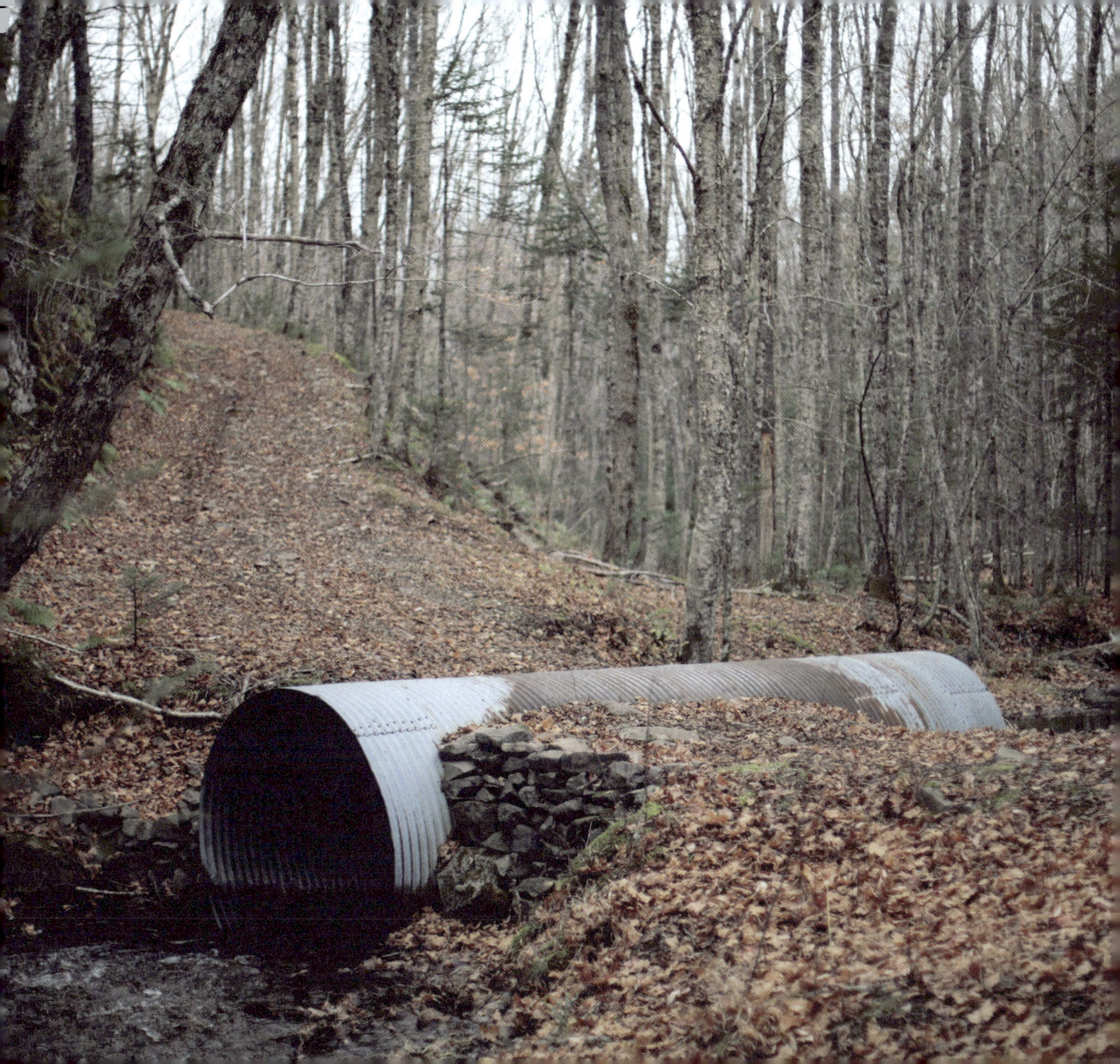

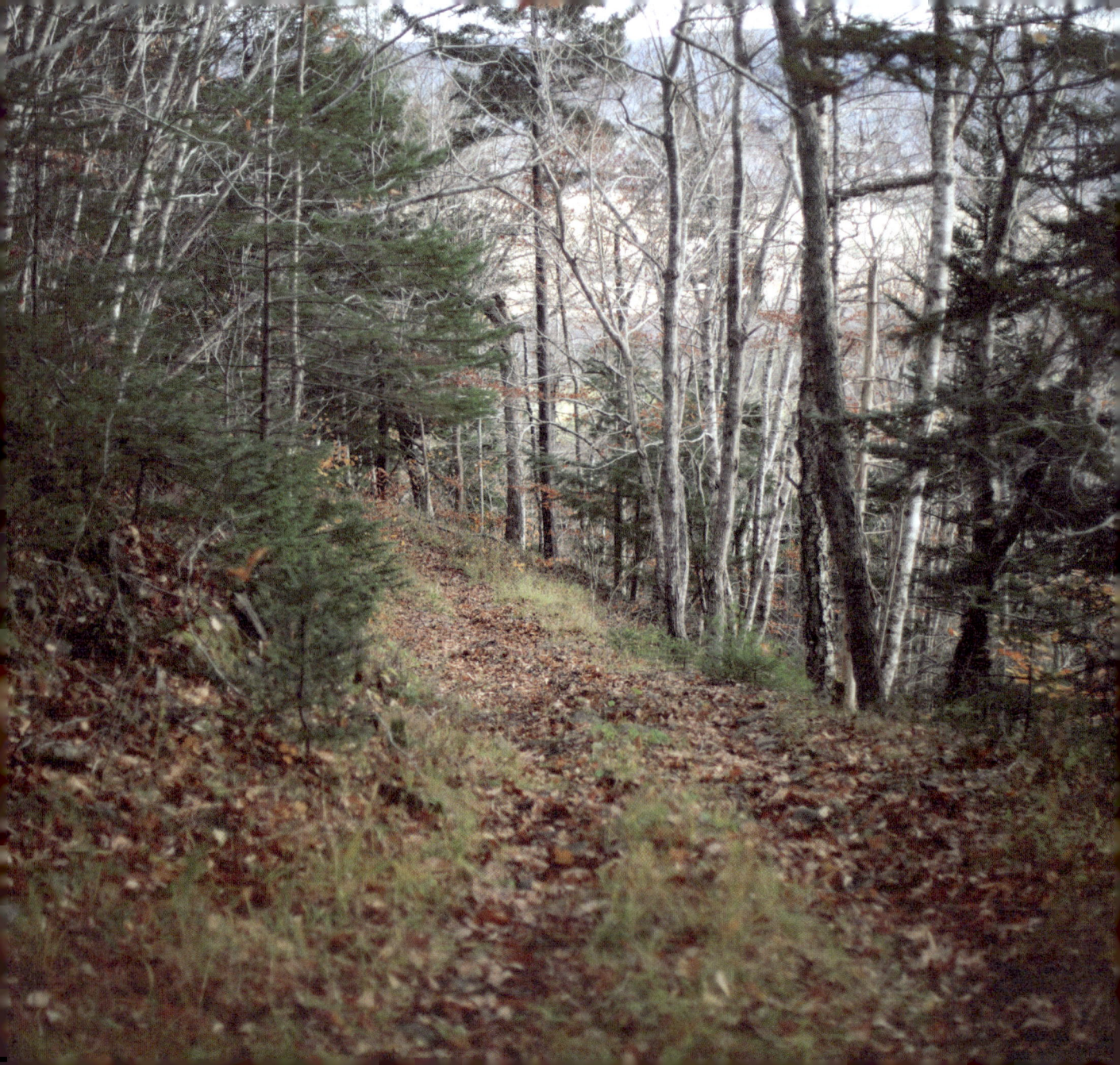

CHUTE ROAD

Beaconsfield, Annapolis County

This road is just one of the many mountain paths that once connected Annapolis Valley to Bay Shore, bridged the rocky gap between a winding river and the roaring ocean—ending in the community of Chute's Cove, modern-day Hampton. Less than two kilometres west of my childhood home, this is a road we hiked as kids. I was just five when we first came here. I was the smallest then, barely visible under layers of warmth against the chill. A picture exists of us bundled tightly, shuffling through snow to a summit we never reached, turned back by the blizzard.

For decades since, I've said I'd return, finally climb to the top, and round the ridge that's been buzzing in my memory so long. Can't say exactly why it never happened, put off while I wandered just about everywhere else in my homeland. A couple years back, I came halfway in from the shore side. Now, I've finally returned, kicking rocks all the way up a steep slope. Looking down on the world like an ant colony below, feeling like the adventurer I always did in places like these. If I'd known back then who I'd become, nothing would've made me happier. All I've ever wanted was to make my young self proud.

I finally found the forgotten fireplace after a couple of years spent seeking out a story, working off nothing but a little oral history, tracking neighbours' tales through bitter rains and heatwave evenings. I was luckless over several summers, but I'm calling

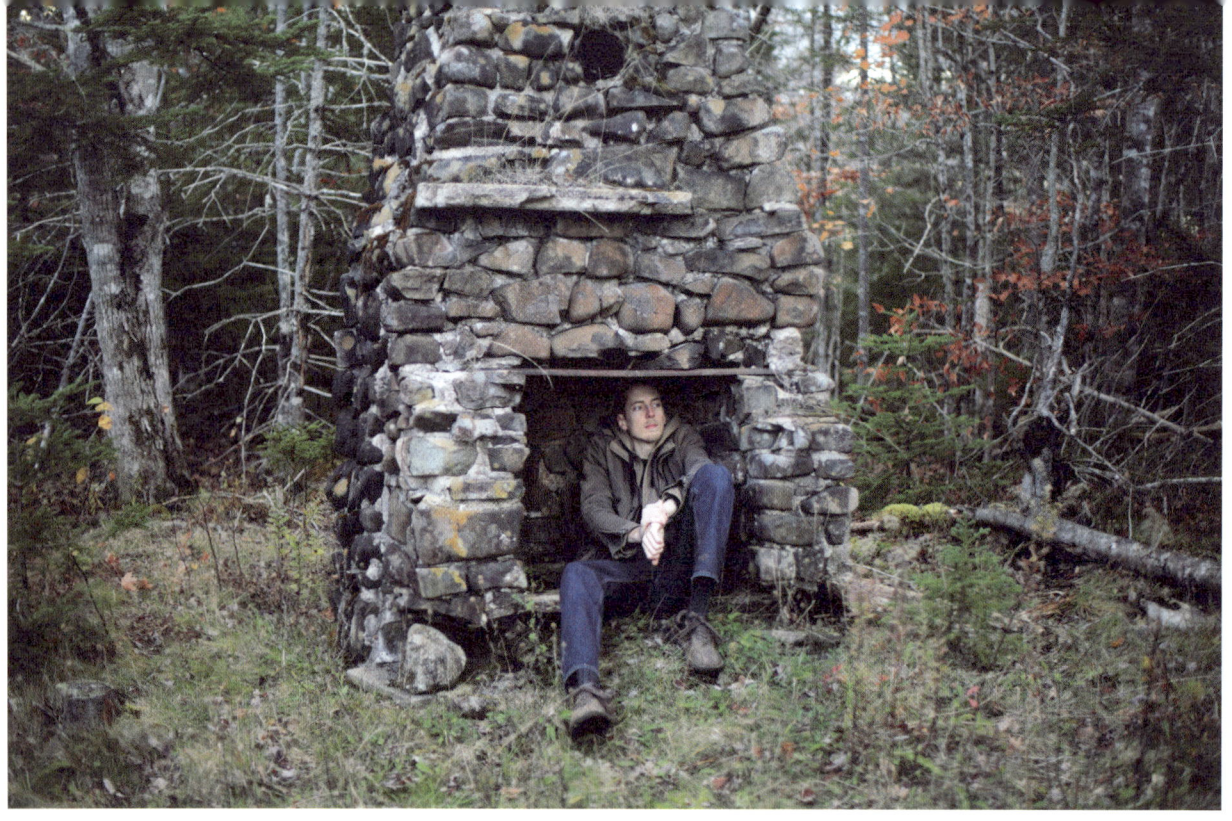

here home for the chill—the stones shed no warmth, but I still feel the fire. Whisked off with dead day-dreaming down one of the many side trails, it was built by some folks who thought their future here. No one seems to know who they were for certain. Some say hippies or draft dodgers, others claim it dates back many generations before. Either way, they went around hoping, like we're all tempted, trying on a sigh for size. Equally unknown is just who placed the more recent signpost near the switchback saying: On Your Way to Mountain Top-Time.

Halfway up the climb is a massive landslide that almost took out Chute Road. I make things like these metaphors for me, since my grip on being grounded

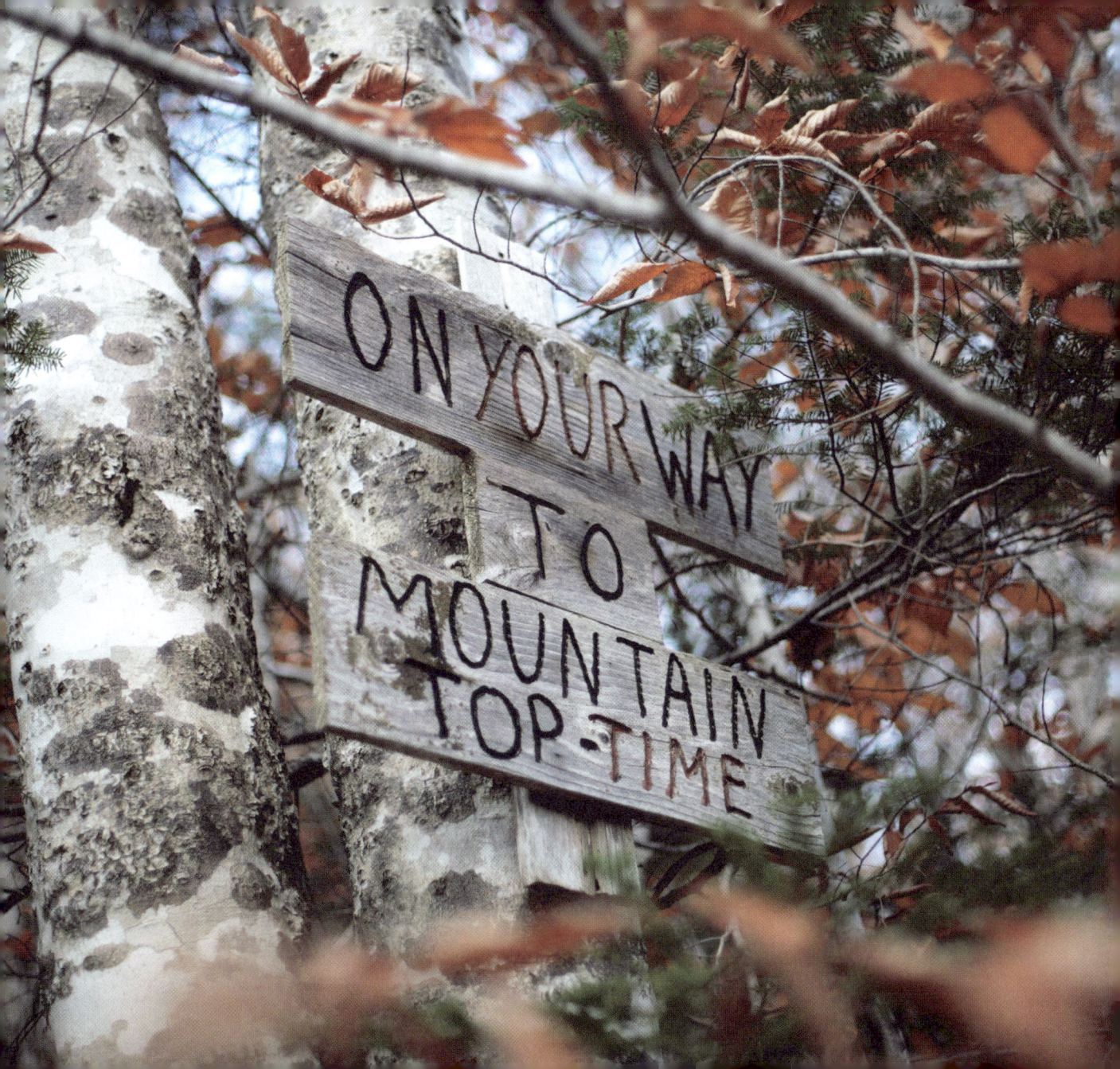

has always been shifting. I remember my late teens in Beaconsfield as a mass of years when I'd buy up any belief. If it looked a little like love, good enough, even if she never appealed to me. If it seemed like a chance to make my way, it was soon a sure thing, until I woke one morning and knew I'd been deluded. By the time I drifted a little nearer to reality, I'd learned how to hope with direction, pointed down a road with a reason in mind. When I started my daily journal, soon after my twentieth birthday, it was no clear clue where I was headed. But I would've been happy knowing it was my ticket up, from tired old ashes I'd left my heart in. Seventeen years later, and I haven't missed a day, but I never miss one once it's gone.

44.85373, -65.32920

5.6 kilometres. Runs north up the mountain from Clarence Road to Shore Road West. Park on the shoulder of the maintained section.

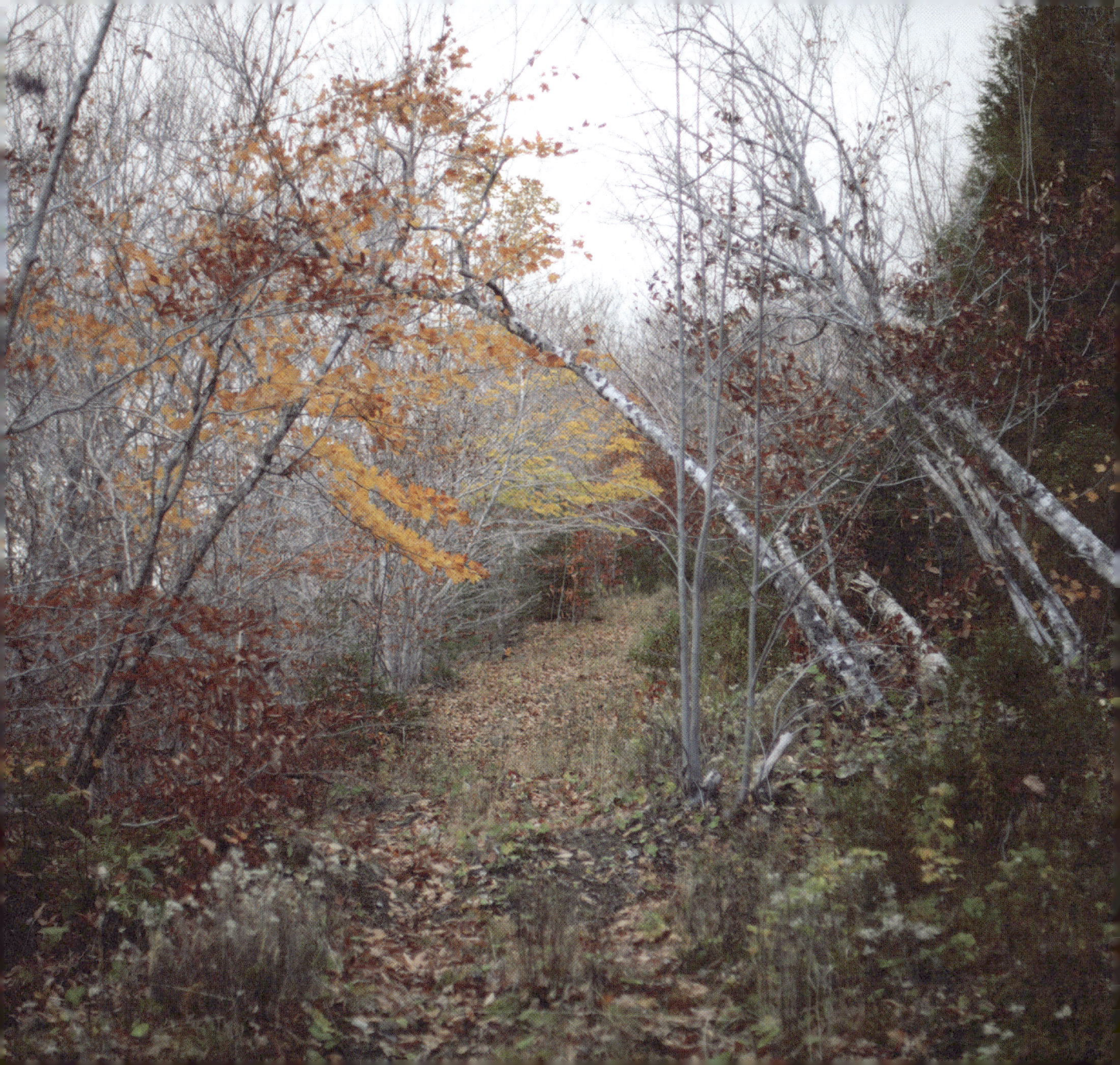

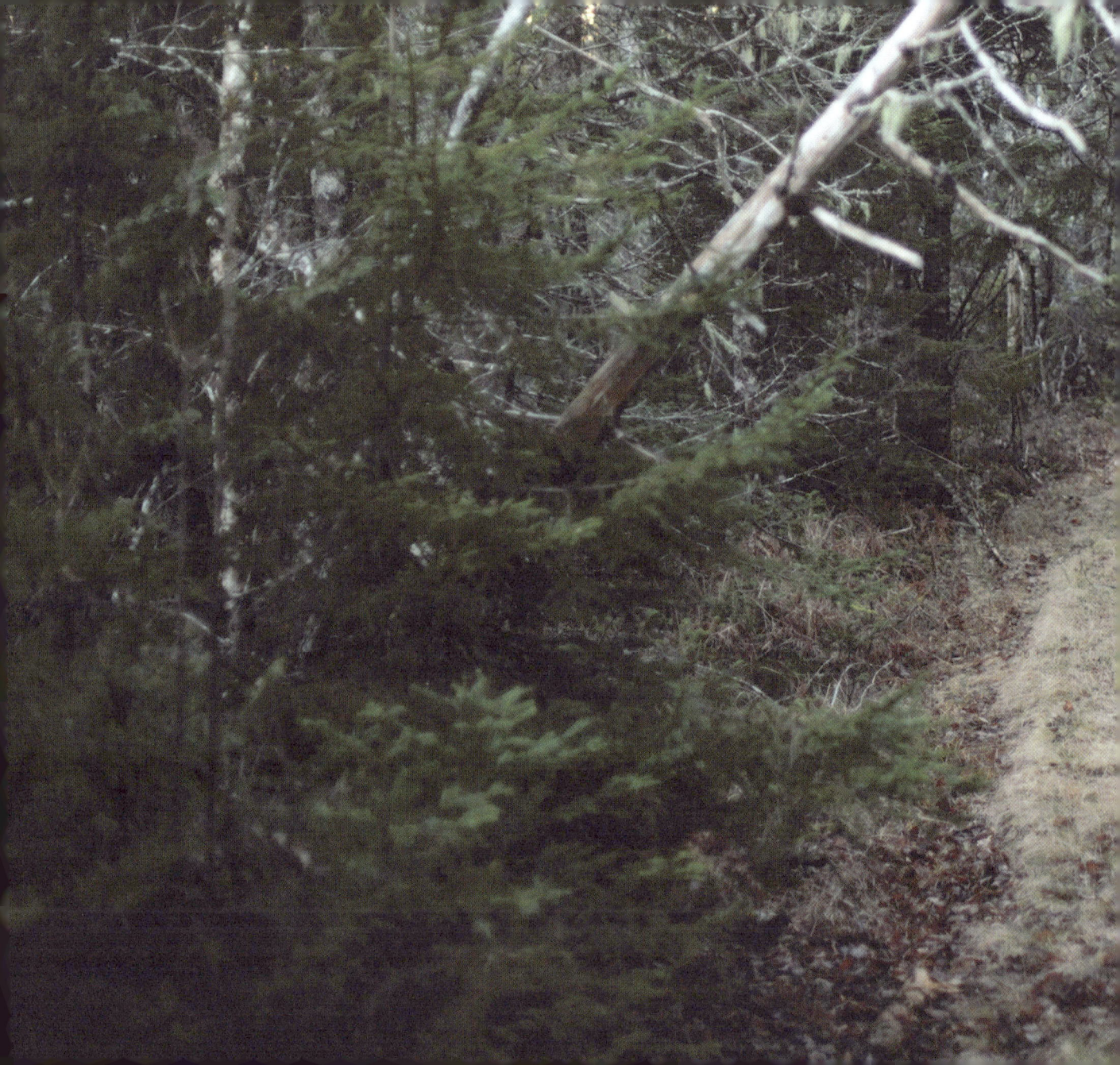

CHAPTER 2

Winter Is a Long Time to Dream

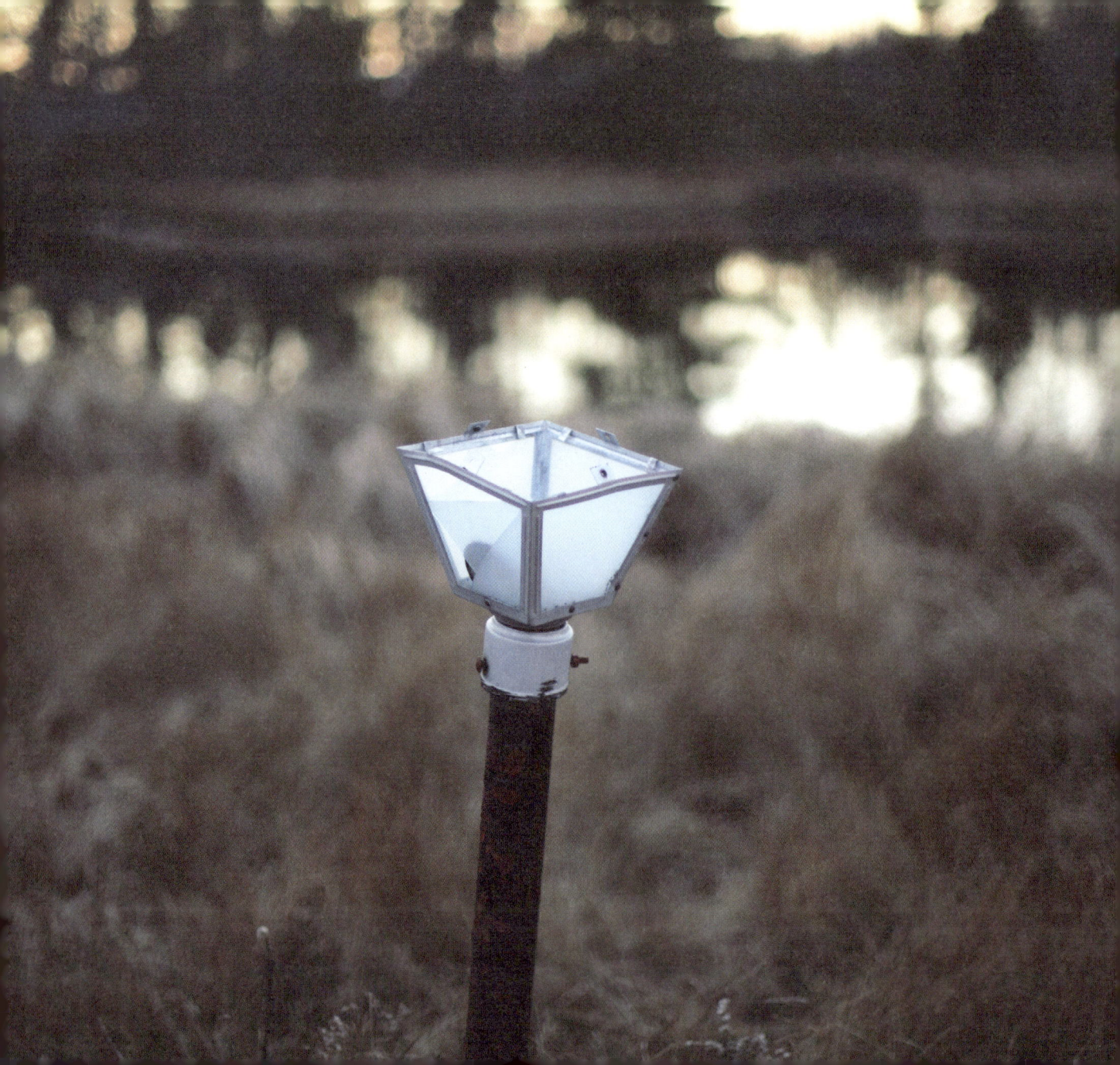

BEN RITCEY ROAD

Stanley Section, Lunenburg County

I feel the come-along signs of daydreaming at the mouth of this derelict road, along a row of broken lights, calling to carry me down to the woods. The curves and bends of Ben Ritcey are mostly low and swampy, just high enough over the waterline to keep your feet from getting wet. So we slip off now and whisper deep, from the shattered street lamps of the long-lost Birch Pond Drive-In on Lower Branch Road, through the trees and over Sheridan Brook, Manning Brook, eventually out to Osborne Road. Between here and there is history, grown over and crumbling. Ruts that hit heavy underfoot cut sharp and solid like rollercoaster tracks, always shouldering you back in. There are birds who sing while I sometimes listen, and a darkness that never stops drawing in at the edges. I cover ground quicker all the while. Slow at first as afternoon lingers, then headlong through what's left of the light. No artificial shine in this place anymore, I owe myself to the sun and sun only.

In the fall of late autumn, I'm always pulled to the edge of darkness. Every day, no fail and no surprise, I follow my feet into twilight. The late woods have no shadows, just a growing gloom from curtains of clouds and some sunset on a far horizon. It's the dangling stick that draws me, a carrot come-and-get-it, the hunger of adventure anywhere I haven't been. There's an old rock dam about halfway down this road, long gone in the middle, maybe the site of some old sawmill. I

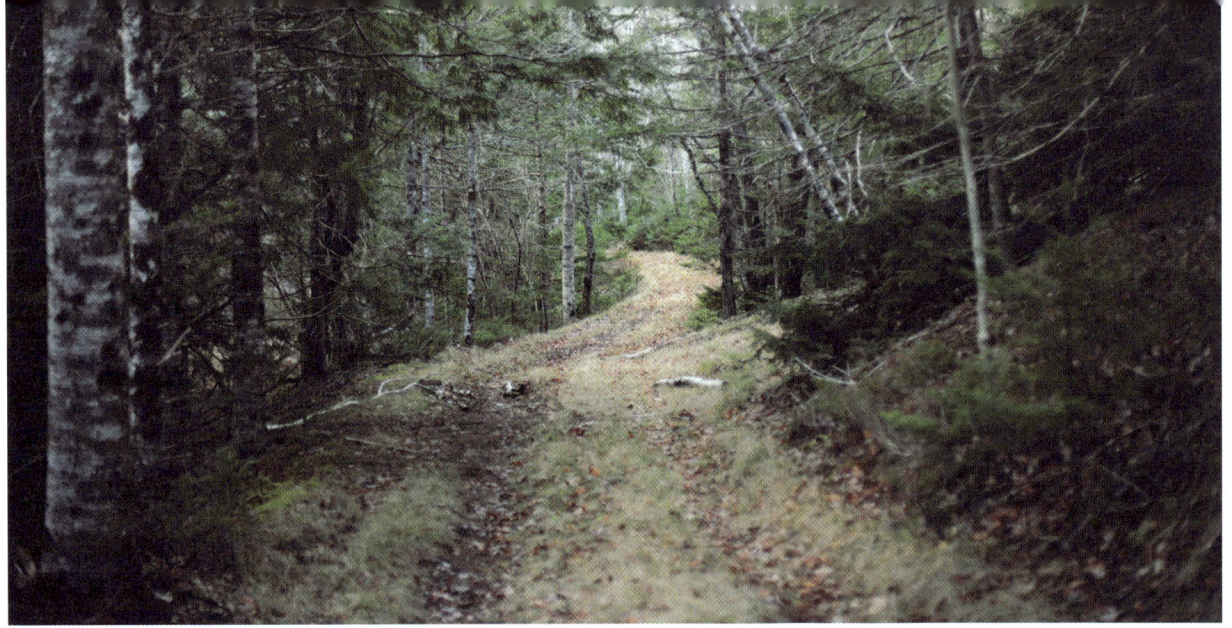

can almost hear the ghostly rattle and buzzing, the lumber led off and crashing, the rough-handed, red-necked men shouting. I'm nothing like them, tied to work that just might kill them, all dead now by any estimation. I just want to wander down the murky depths of Ben Ritcey, steady in search of the past.

44.51255, -64.73190

3.3 kilometres. Runs east from Lower Branch Road out to Osborne Road. Park on the shoulder at the mouth of the road.

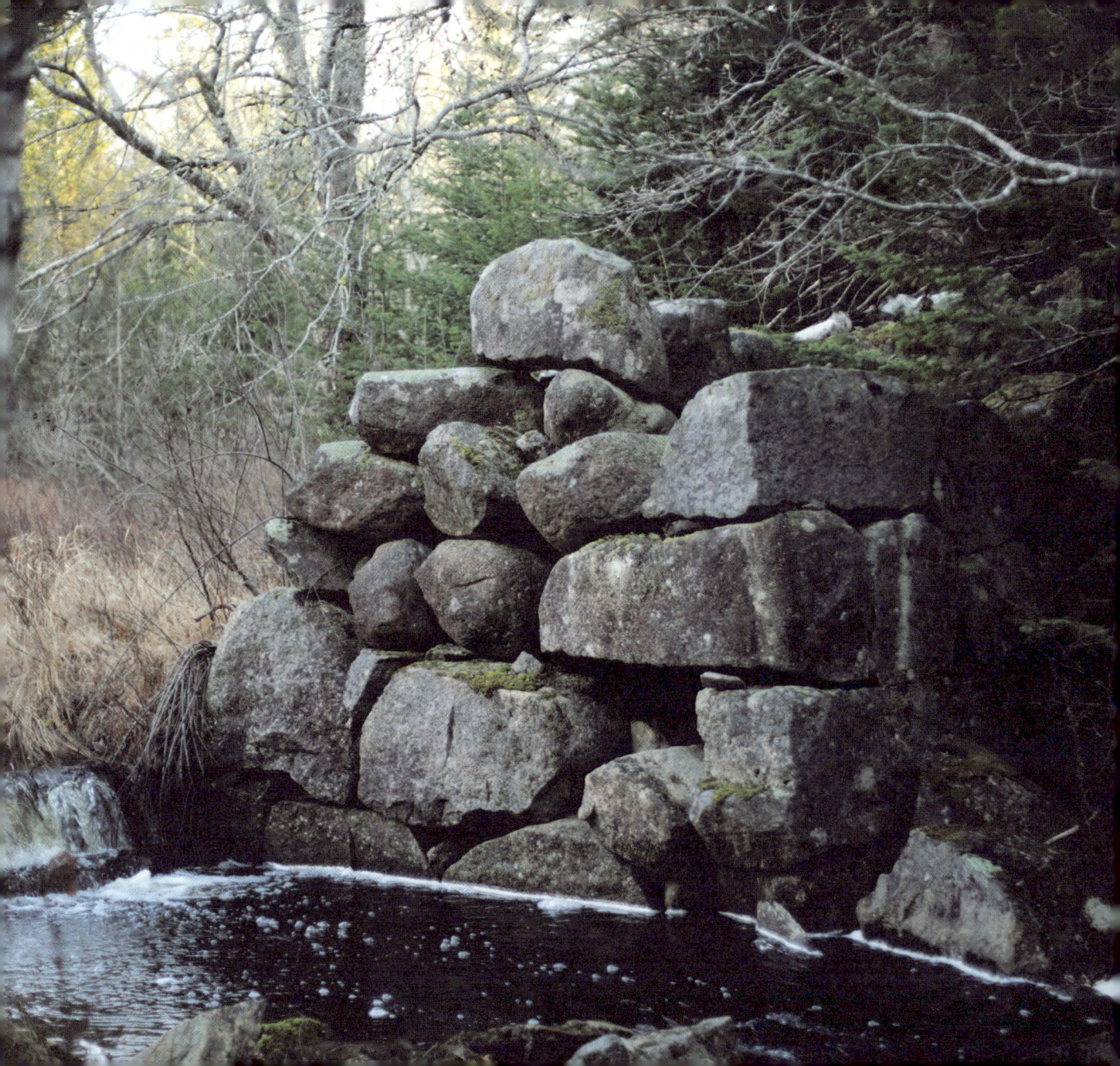

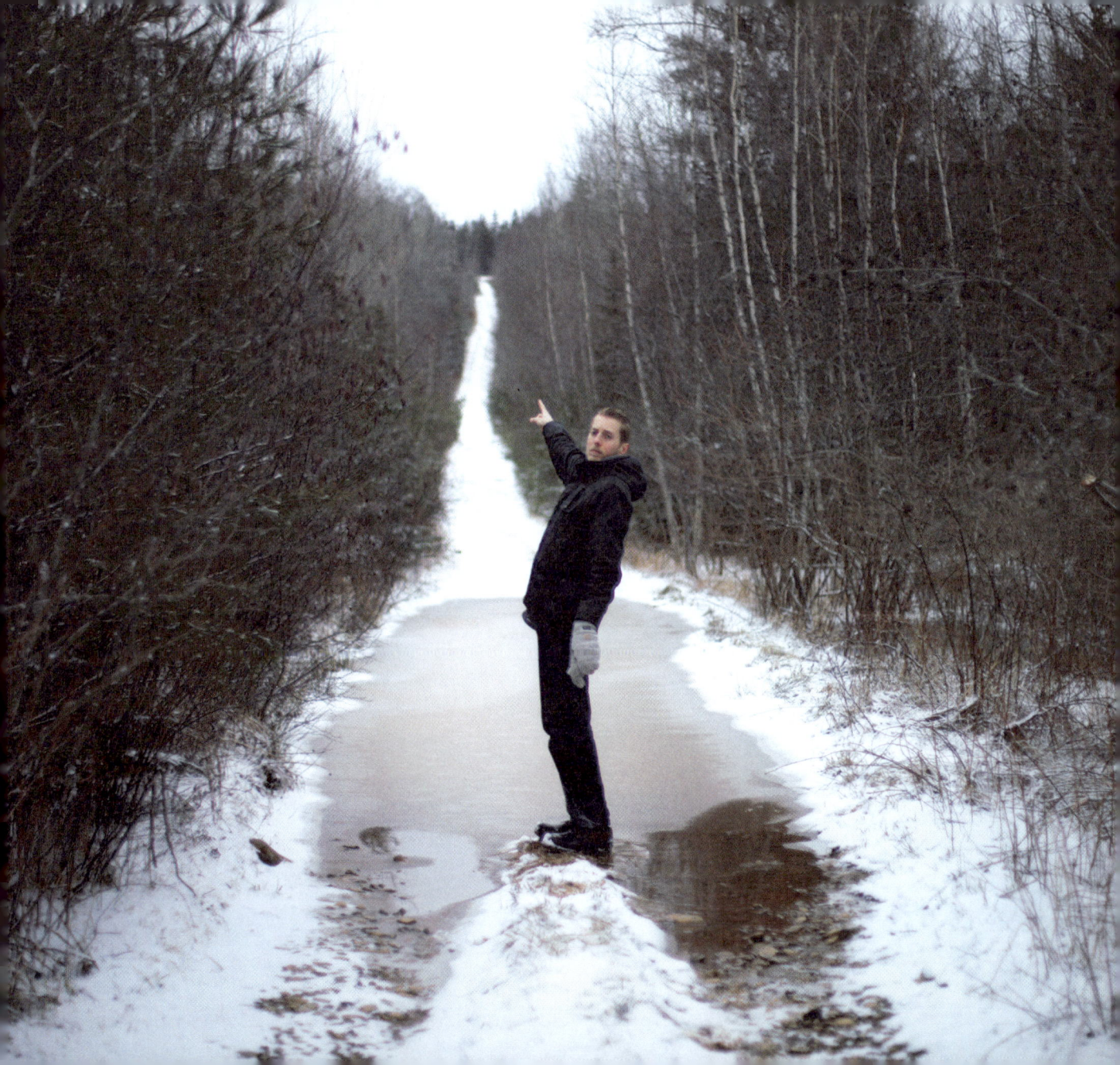

NEILY ROAD

Nictaux South, Annapolis County

Despite the exhaustion and the general brutality of the experience, I never regret hiking an abandoned road on foot. It's a long way down off South Mountain, from the fields on high through the washed-out woods below. There was a time when these forests were well settled, cleared from top to bottom for the various scattered homesteads. The pioneers were Parker, Saunders, Jones, and Willet. It took a whole lot of bushwhacking, and bushes whacking me back, but I was able to find a few of their ancient foundations in the brush. First was the one for E. Parker, then P. Saunders, and finally, T. Jones. Their names are scrawled on my map from 1876, and I found their crumbling history right where they left it. Shallow cellars in the earth, a good century or so spent falling inward. Erosion takes everything it can, but somehow, stories keep on growing back.

I've hiked Neily Road a few times before, but I don't know if I will again. With my world so crowded with compelling dereliction, I can always grasp the feeling of when I've added enough of my story to the one that's already there. The up-and-downhill struggle of big distance tests my endurance. I'm no great marathoner, and my circling wandering makes getting anywhere a slow proposition. I get lost in the beauty, a kind of equal alloy between the

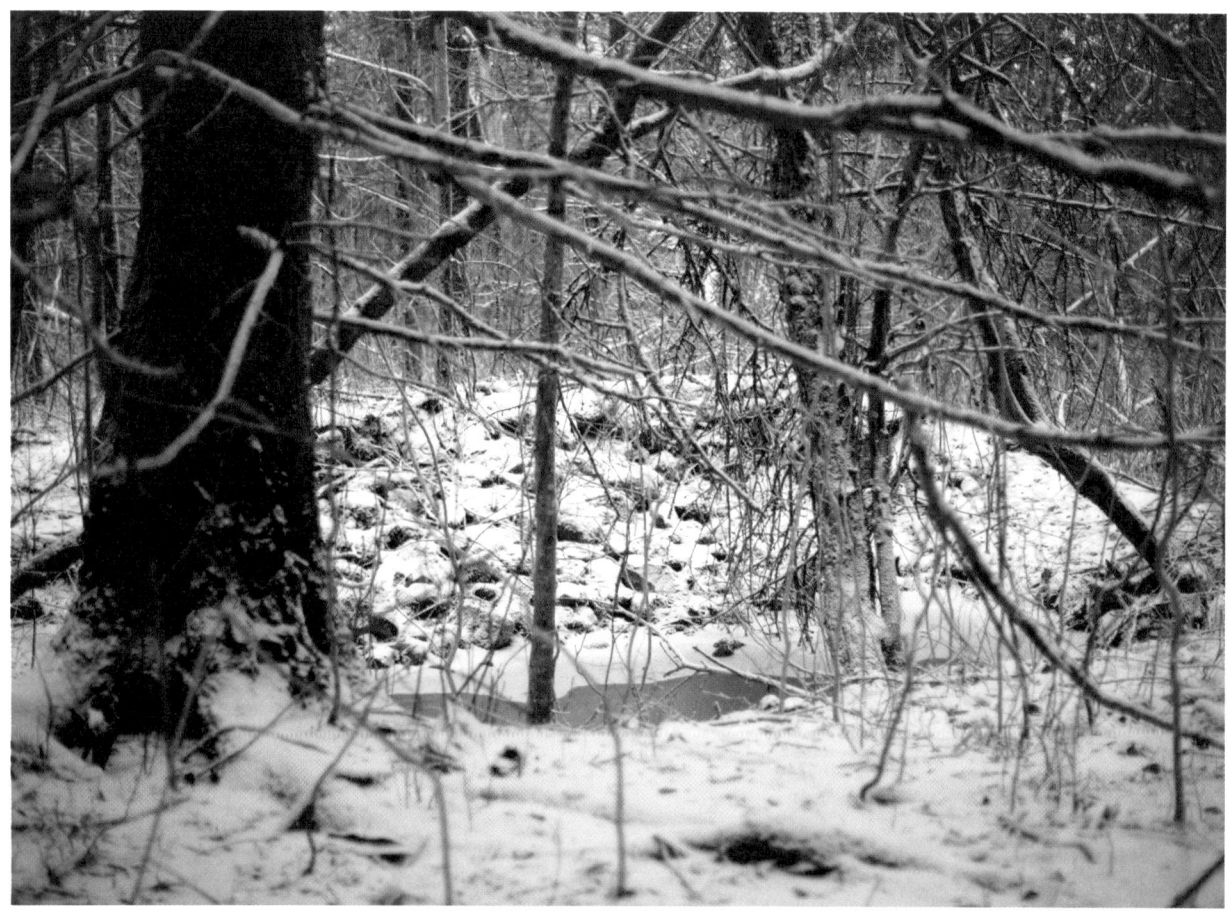

present, past, and the moment that nature is making. Last night, a steady rain settled out to a thin skin of snow—just enough to turn the contours of everything white. Any more would hide all the secrets, any less would cease to exist. There's a sober sort of drunkenness I feel for this wet-chill weather.

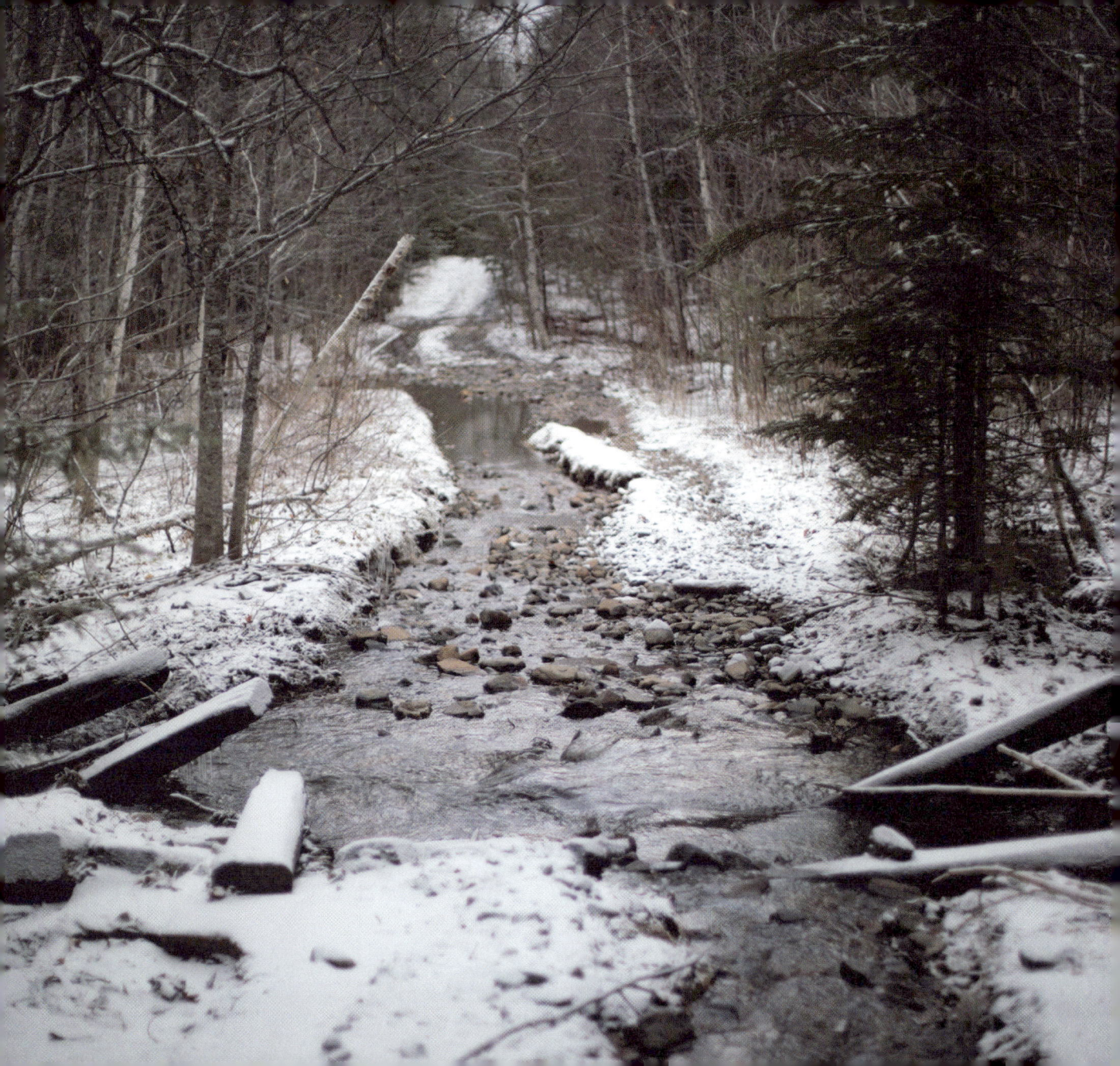

Spun around in tribute to the spell that cold casts, tracking out the ruts that still hold their ancient width. I walk on a little deeper to where the washouts gather lower. This river was once a road, and I'm riding those rapids all the way back.

44.88210, -65.04379

4.0 kilometres. Runs briefly west after Civic #205, then goes north until the road is maintained again near Highway 201. Park on the shoulder.

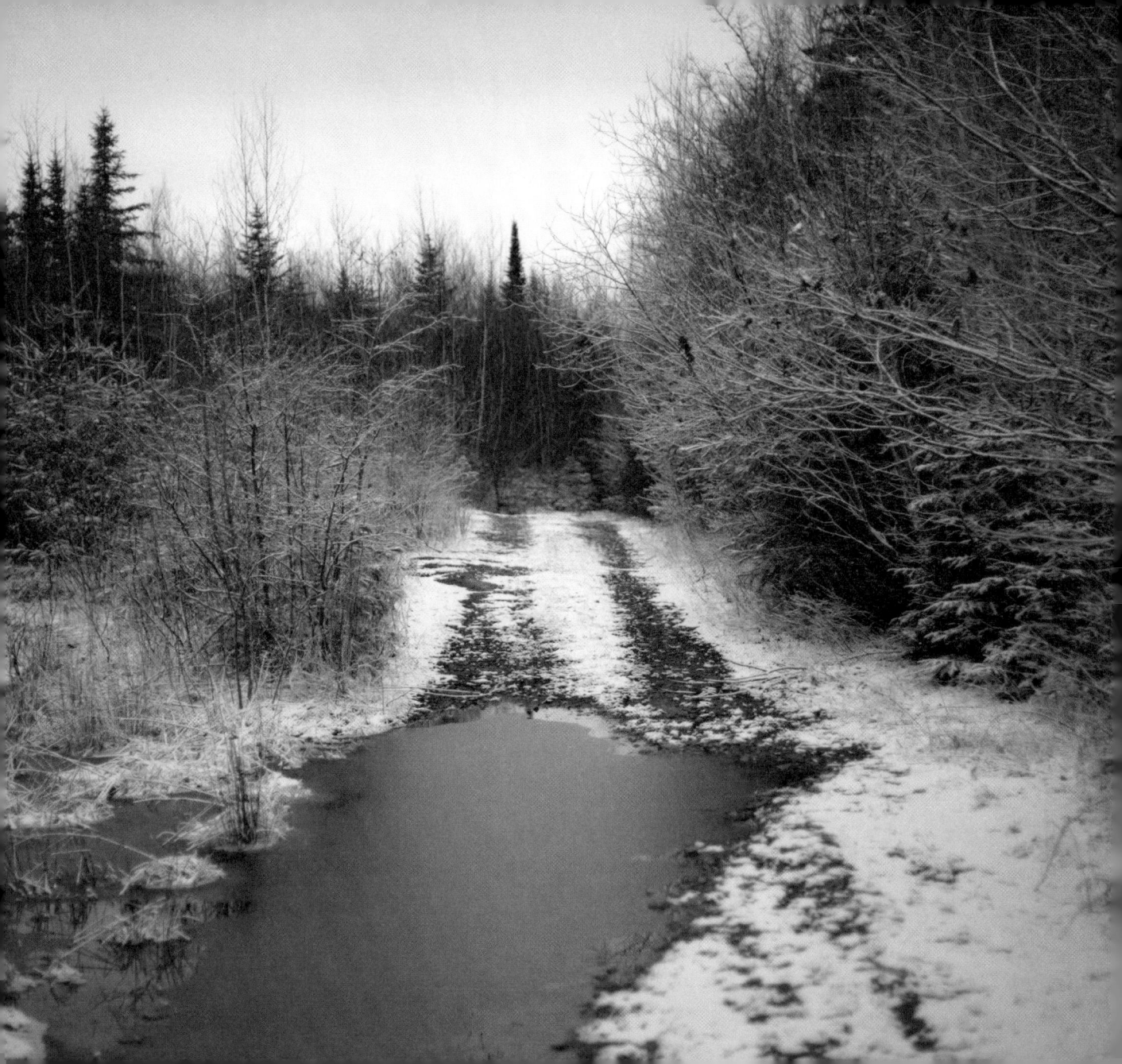

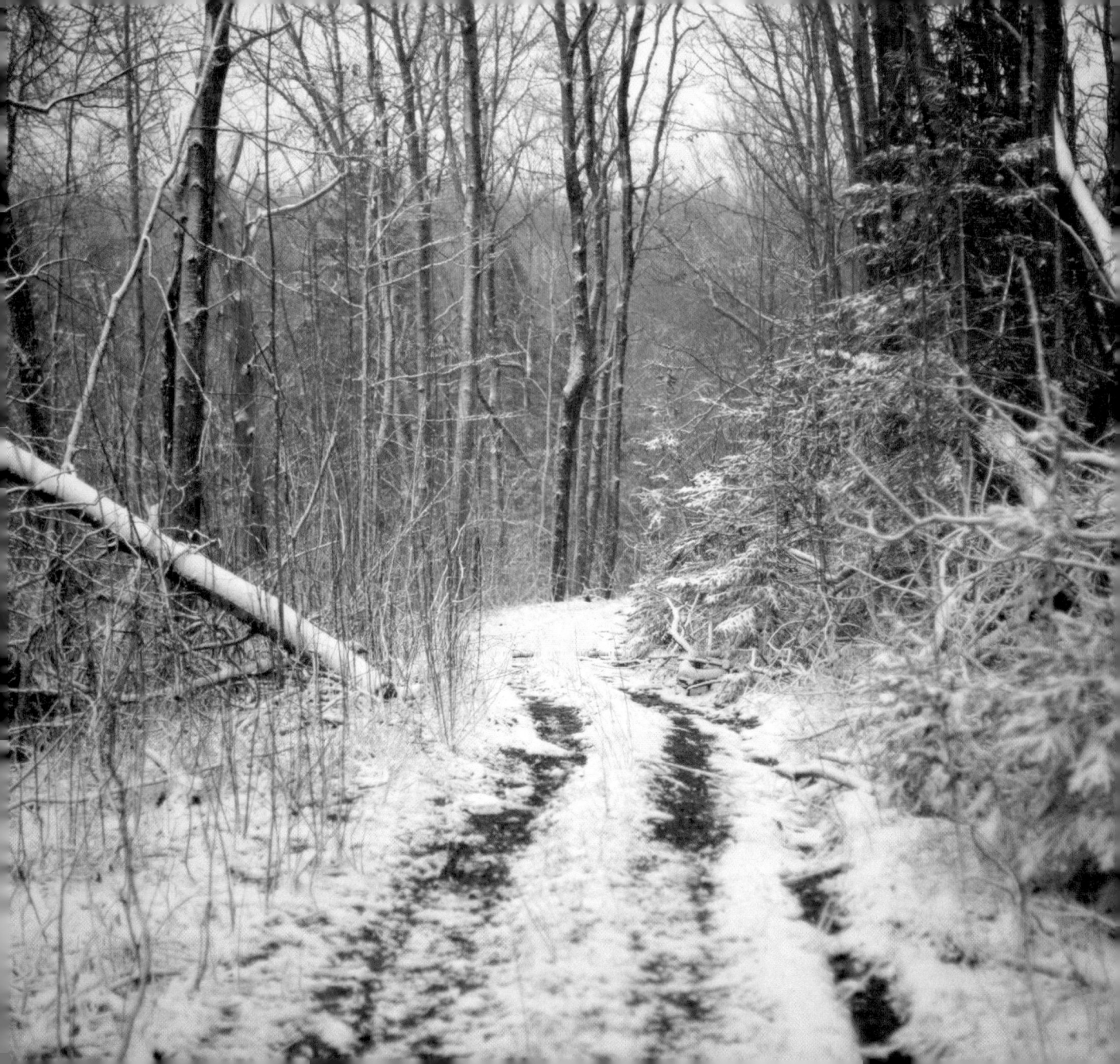

ALPENA ROAD

Nictaux South, Annapolis County

A surprise snow on the edge of spring is always otherworldly, wet flakes falling and getting stuck on every surface. It's just cold enough to not be raining, making me feel for a minute like I'm back in autumn. These are the limbo weeks when I'm never quite certain, spotting wildflowers one day, chilled to the bone the next. I went on a hike through the woods to the old Nova Scotia Central Railway, now just a gravel bed on the banks of the Nictaux River. Down here hides the rush of the Alpena Rapids, crashing rocks on a northern passage to the Valley floor.

This abandoned road looks pretty straight on the map, but underfoot, curves always keep the mystery intact. You never know what's next for more than thirty seconds at once, everything revealed and shrouded again, bend after bend. I look at every hike in terms of effort and reward. This one isn't so long, has an old homestead site and a dam, and ends at the railbed and river soon after. The towering trees remind me how derelict roads are defined by nature. So long as they stand, it feels like an adventure. Take them down and it all falls apart.

Old human-planted trees are some of the most beautiful things in the forest, standing strangely separate from the rest of the woods, growing in perfectly planned rows. Nearby lie the remnants of lives—a

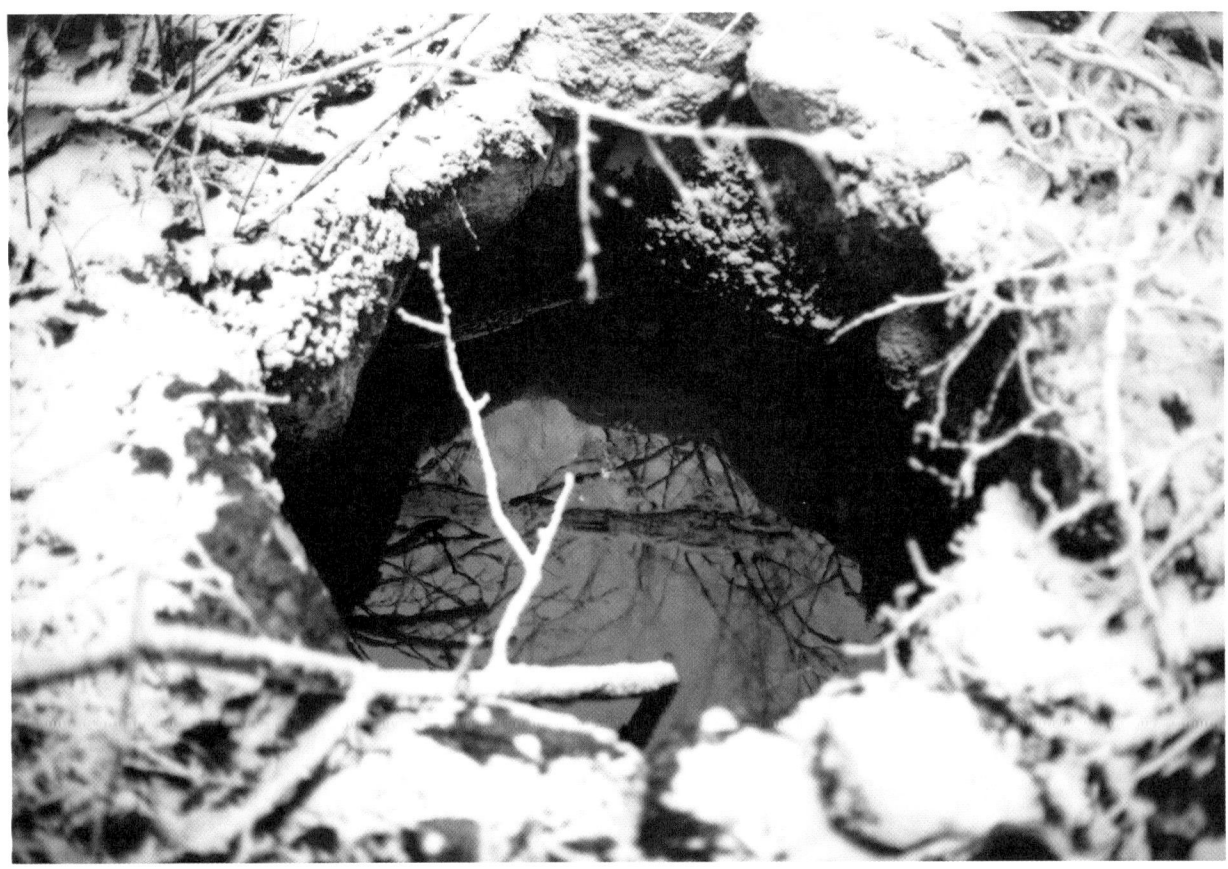

vacant foundation, an open well, a concrete dam that turned this stream into a pond. The families of Gates and Dunn still leave their lingering marks. While this sprawling monster of a tree holds sway and shade here, few visitors stop to settle under. But I've never hiked this abandoned road as a stranger, always drawn to the ancient tendrils of trunks spilling out on the banks. A late snow illuminates, like light on every

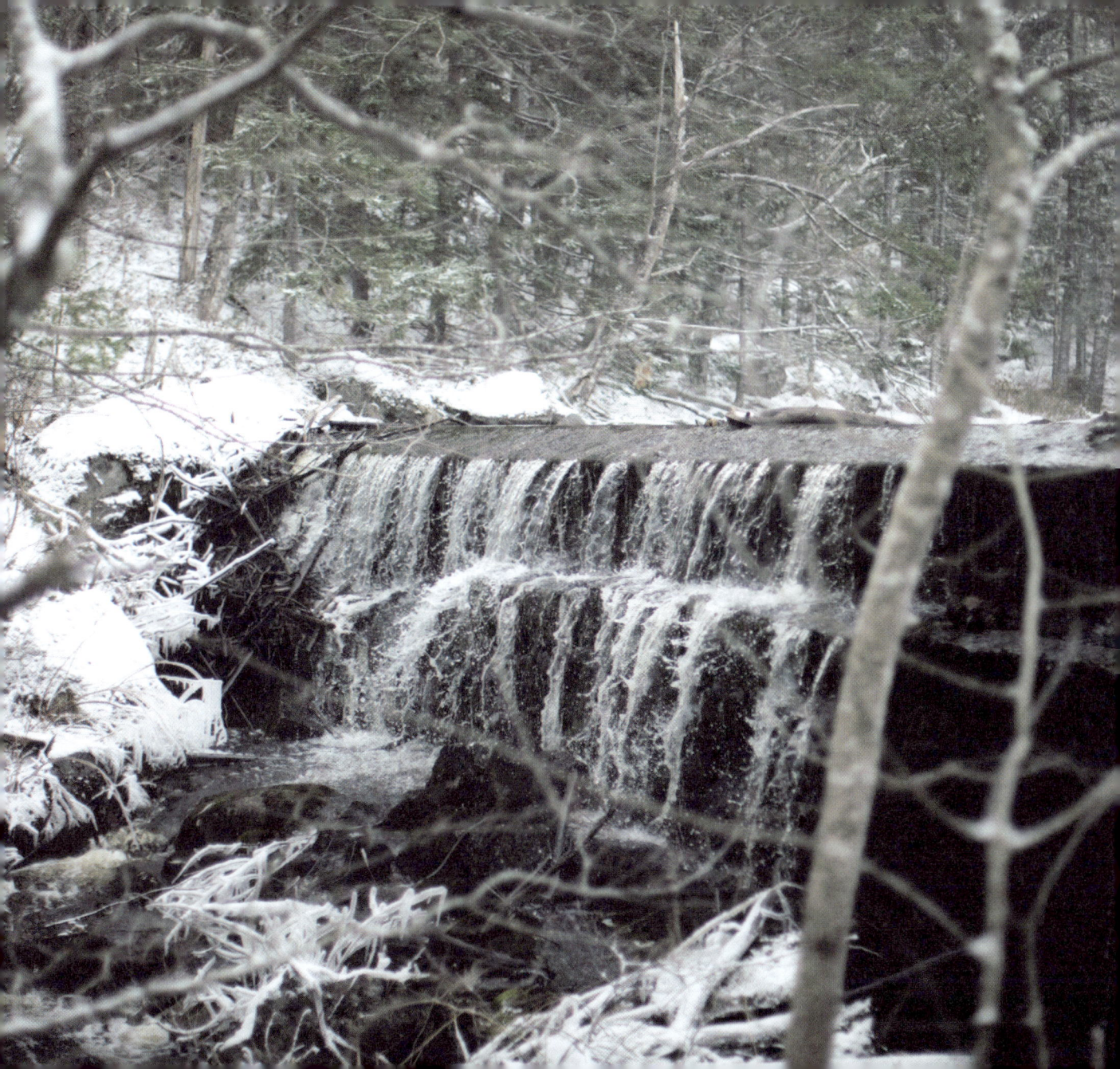

twig, white silhouettes of young growth spreading, still sure signs of life in the coming season. One of the horrors in human aging is when we stop growing and still survive, but nature knows nothing of it. There is always only up, aiming for sunlight until the end. No less alive until everything is over, and even surrender is against our will. I try to be like trees.

44.84181, -65.05539

1.5 kilometres. Runs southeast from Highway 10 down to the railbed and Nictaux River. Park on the shoulder of the maintained section.

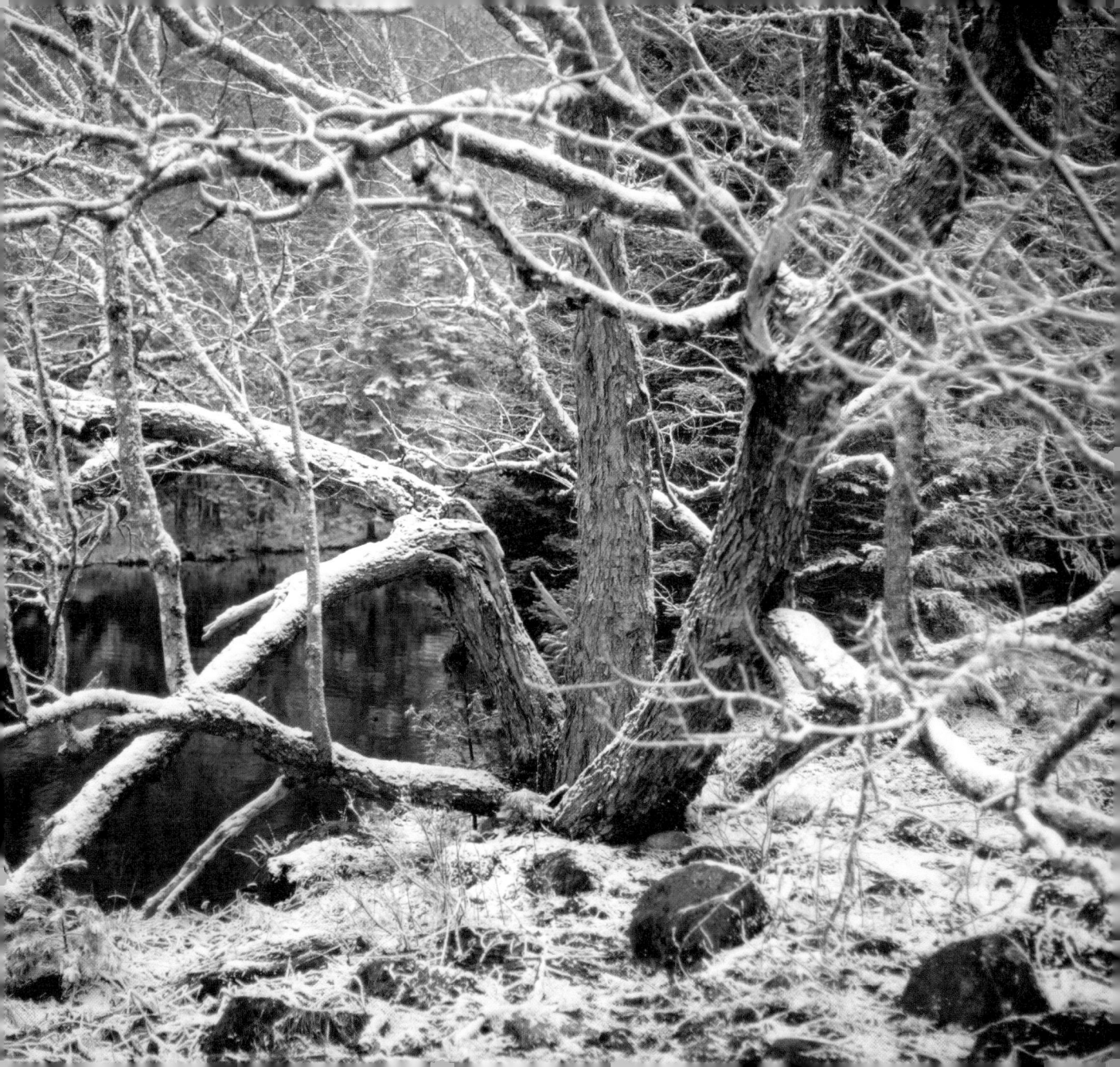

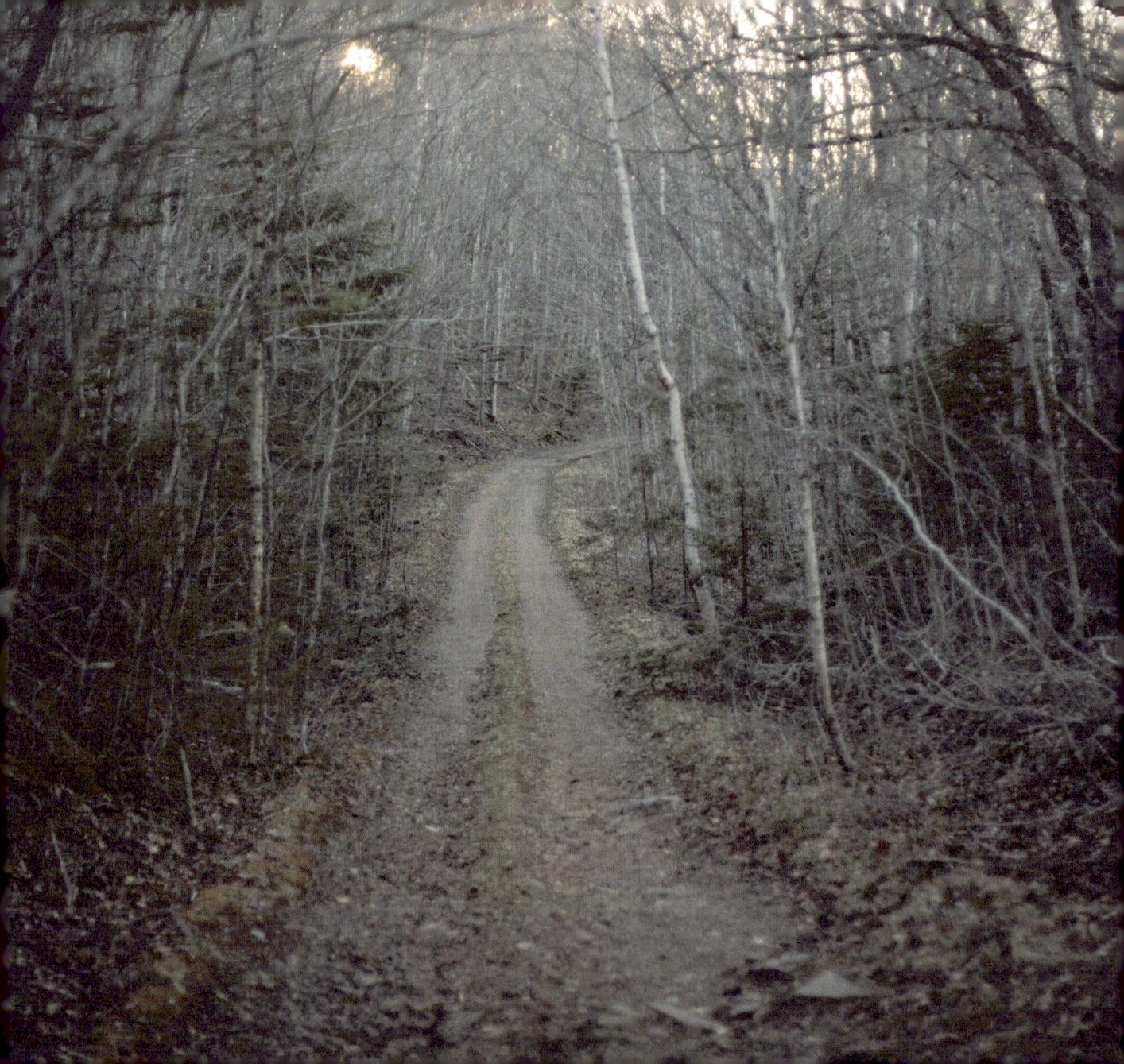

DODGE ROAD

Spa Springs, Annapolis County

Hiking into twilight is a beautifully unnerving sensation. I rarely do it anywhere new, but I'd made this mountain pass many times before. Josiah and Benjamin Dodge were the earliest settlers, responsible for making a way through these woods. Their narrow trail has a ghostly feeling about it—crowded curves and bends carrying centuries of travellers before. No one settled on high in the early days, and no one since. No need, with fertile land in the Valley behind and The Vault below. That latter hollow peeks out now and then, with a view of working farms through bare branches in a sinking sight below. These ridges are rocky and windswept, and roots cling for purchase. Right at freezing, steady steps are just enough to push the chill back. Darkness is like a nest that I trust to keep me comforted. I'll make it out just in time for that blue light to fall.

There are few local places with more folklore attached than the deep, dark space known as "The Hole in The Vault." I'd sought this place for years, off and on, picking along the slippery slopes between Vault and Dodge Roads. Now and then, someone would offer vague directions, rarely more helpful than narrowing down a general area—information I already knew. Most folks hadn't even been there themselves. Coming up empty after a dozen searches, I decided to give it one last shot before heavy rain made mud and rocks too slippery to scale. This time, I

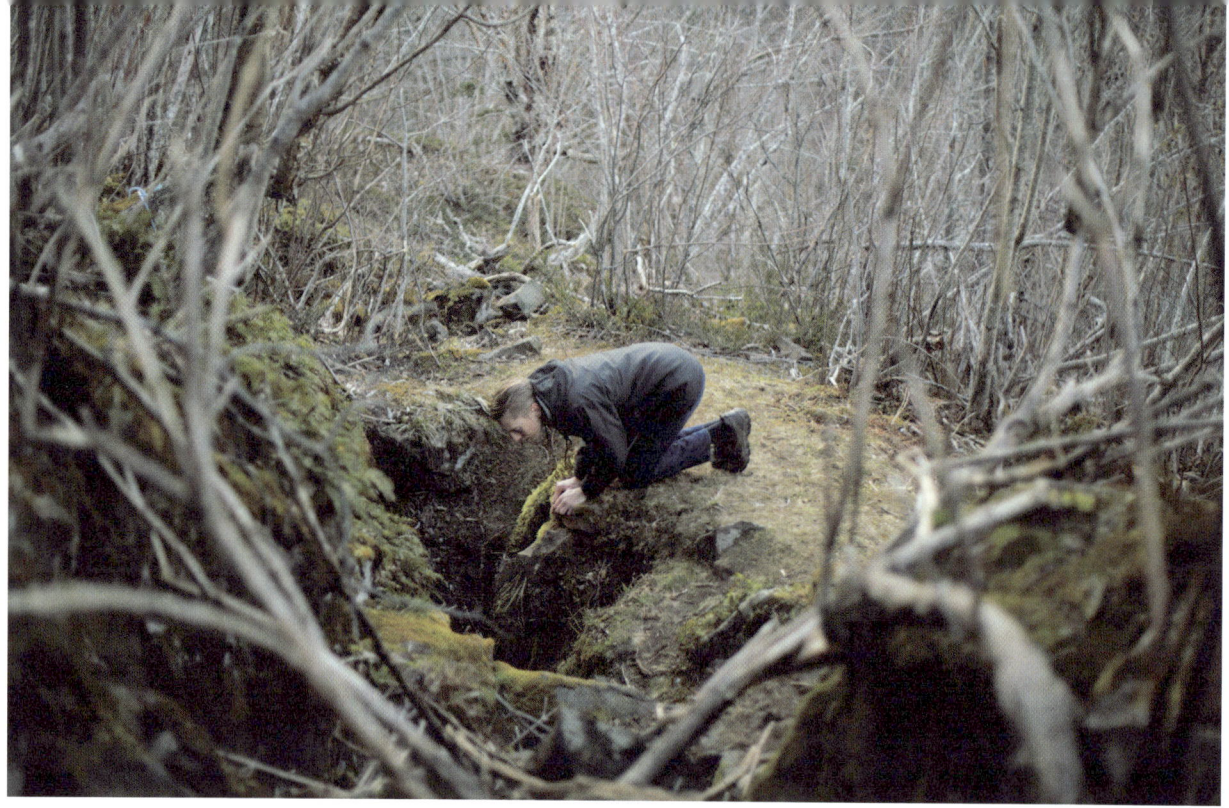

followed topographic maps made recently with lidar, aiming through brush to the sharpest outcropping I could find.

Deep in the woods between Melvern Square and Forest Glade, I finally reached a series of jagged fissures along the North Mountain ridgeline. Three narrow slits dropped down into the rock, but only one—a still-icy entryway—continued to a cave. In a somewhat unnerving scenario, it drifts on a shallow diagonal before abruptly plummeting straight down like a well. The first drop is a good twenty feet, and that's just the start of your fall. It's been said that these depths connect to water from the Bay of Fundy, though that's unlikely, with the shore being nearly five kilometres away.

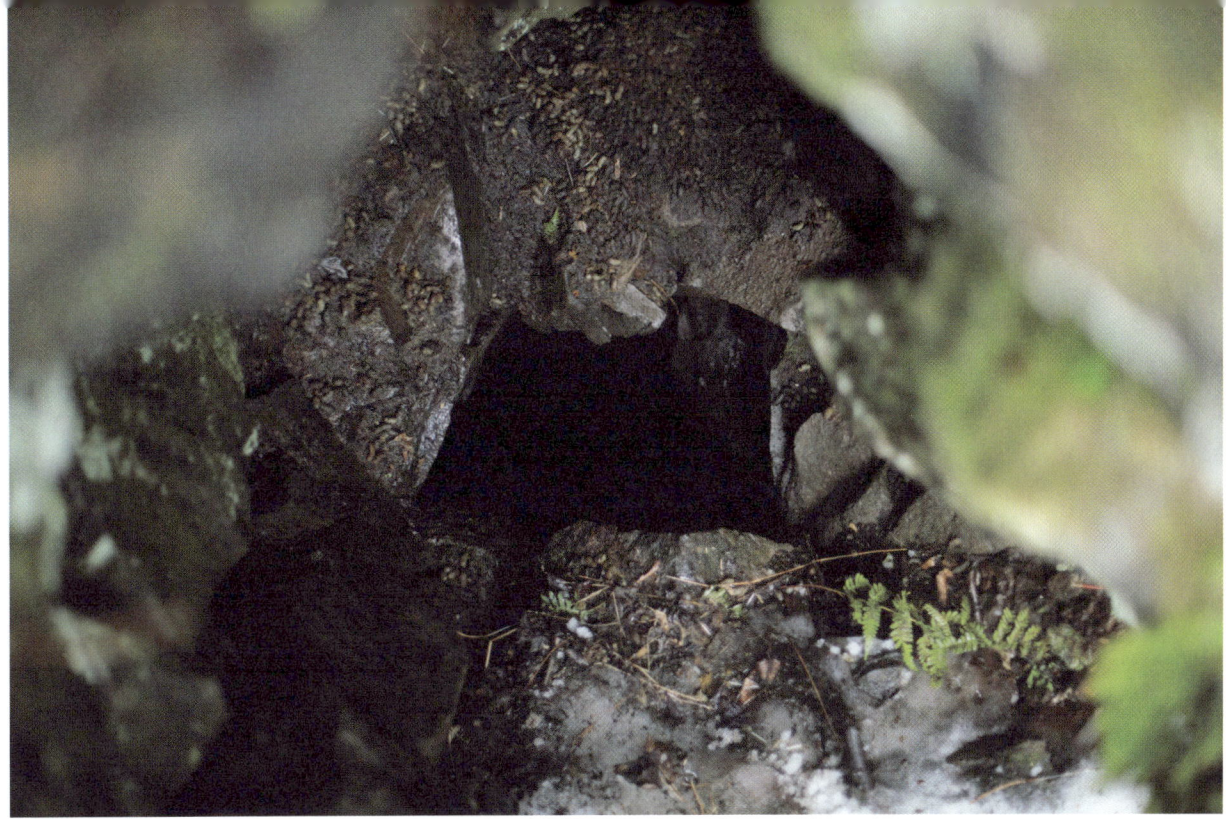

The Hole was first written about in 1892, in a magazine called the *Youth's Companion*. The reporter was Charles G. D. Roberts, a poet. Everything he wrote was secondhand—and here I am, giving it to you third. He was told a tale by one of the three boys who decided to discover just how deep and far the cave could go. After dropping down to an outer gallery, one was strapped to a rope and lowered in a shaft that seemed to have no bottom. A collapse of the walls shattered his headlamp and trapped him for some time, and he nearly didn't make it up. After this incident, local farmers plugged the entrance with trees to prevent further entry. But those have long since rotted away.

I'm no cave diver, and as such, have limited interest in dropping out of sight. It's enough sometimes just to stand on the lip of history, peering into an uneasy past. There will always be someone saying: "Let's go further, let's seek secrets, see what the shadows are keeping from us." Tonight, I learned that porcupines are an active part of that. Their droppings scattered in thousands, stinking like mud; babies chirping discontentedly at my disturbance. Hundreds of feet from this vantage, the view across The Vault is breathtaking. Stark and leafless, mostly muted of the outside world. You couldn't feel more alone for trying. My legs were burning by the time I came back to my car—and I felt content for finally finding one more secret that the wild was keeping.

44.98835, -65.01456

4.5 kilometres. Runs northwest from Civic #830, up the mountain to Forest Glade Road. Park on the shoulder just past the farm.

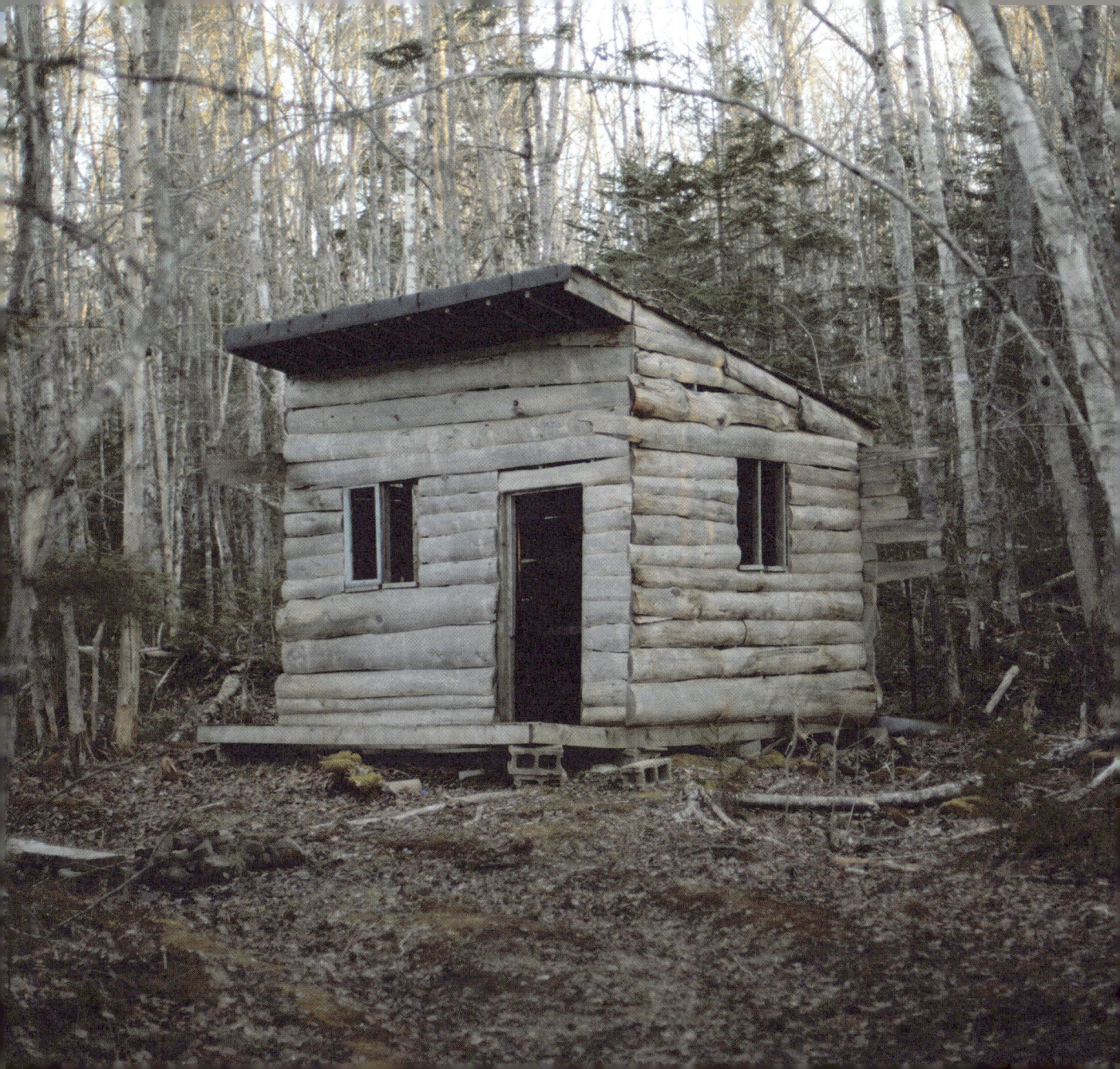

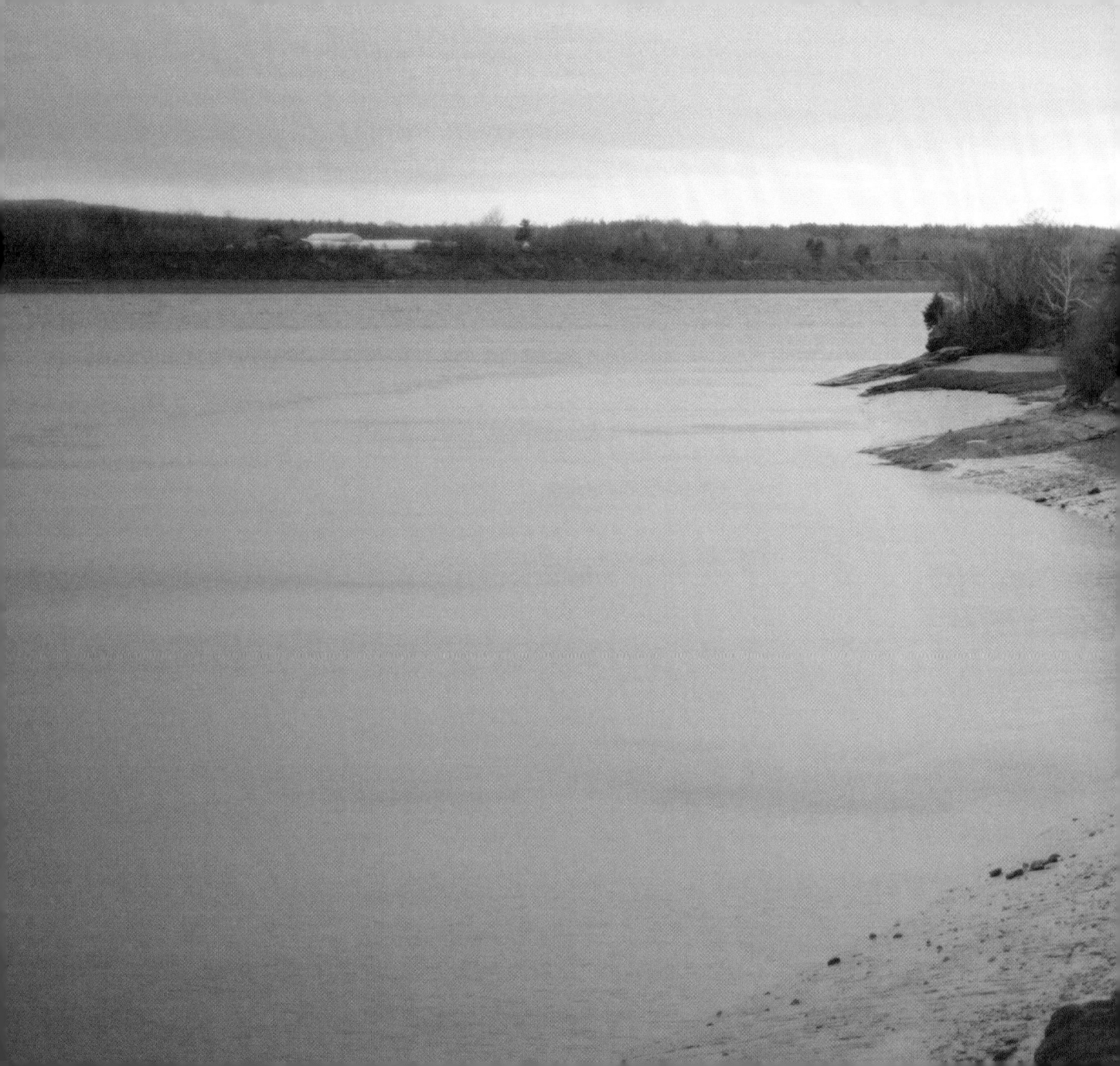

CHAPTER 3

Spring Is a Long Time Coming

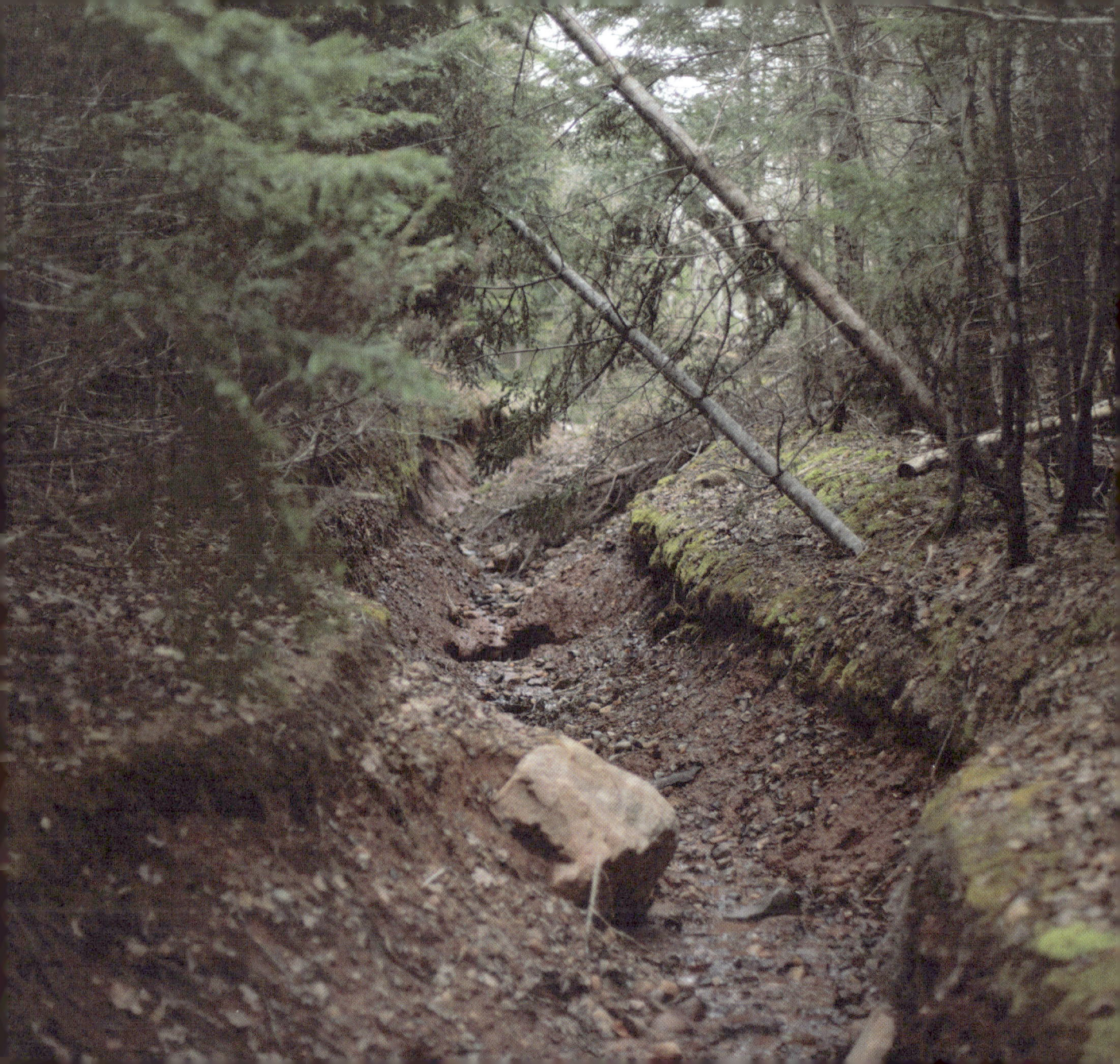

RIVERSIDE ROAD

Princeport, Colchester County

The twisting mystery of this road is all I need tonight, boring its way into my brain as the evening light sinks to meet me. It's equally beautiful and uneasy to go hiking into dark. I really wouldn't recommend it where you've never been before, feeling out the shadowy spaces through the last hours of evening. But I left home on a whirlwind trip with limited funds, escaping east to places I've never seen before. Cash was short, time precious, and every hour underfoot meant the most to fully use. From the rolling fields of Princeport, wandering, through washed-out woods and rock-hopping the trickling Pitch Brook. That little bit of water seemed insignificant to me, but it was named on maps as early as the 1860s, draining down to the Shubenacadie River, rolling deep and out of sight. Tripping ruts like grooves in vinyl, silent lyrics spoken in the words of "was" and "will once more."

When you look on the map, every road seems the same in significance. Sharp lines traced to suggest an easy way through, no sense of scale or hints at the regularity of maintenance. But a long life of sporadic use and impermanent settlement has a way of disseminating the past. These woods were wide-open empty in the overall drift, daydreaming slow and surely, the gap of twilight that hides from those who live a more settled life. I left my car parked at one field and, 2.5 kilometres farther through the wilderness, exited at another. Only those places broken open to the sun showed signs of

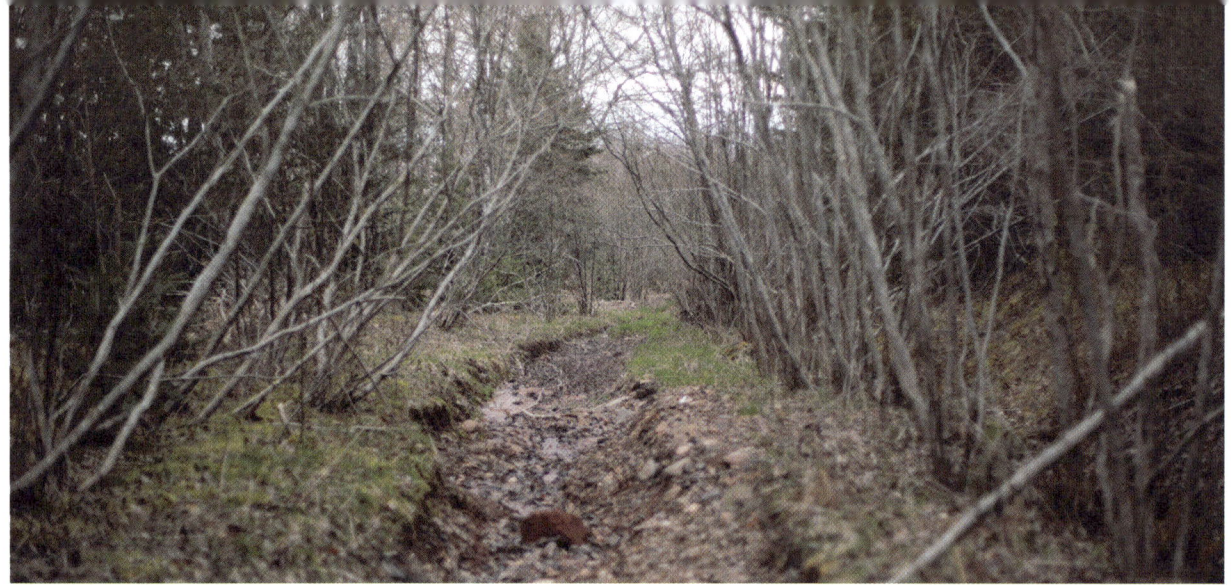

spring, breaking bits of grass and weed that the deeper spaces didn't suggest. The skyline split to muddy cliffs eroding down the banks of "Shubie," slowly working at sinking the land to sea level. The return journey was made in near-dark. I finally left the woods in a murky half-haze, the kind that's shaped from a mist made only of my own night vision. The rest is blinking back the ghosts in periphery.

45.29732, -63.46670

2.5 kilometres. Runs north 120 metres past Civic #4499, crossing Pitch Brook, ending at the next active farmland along Shubenacadie River. Park on the shoulder at the mouth of the field.

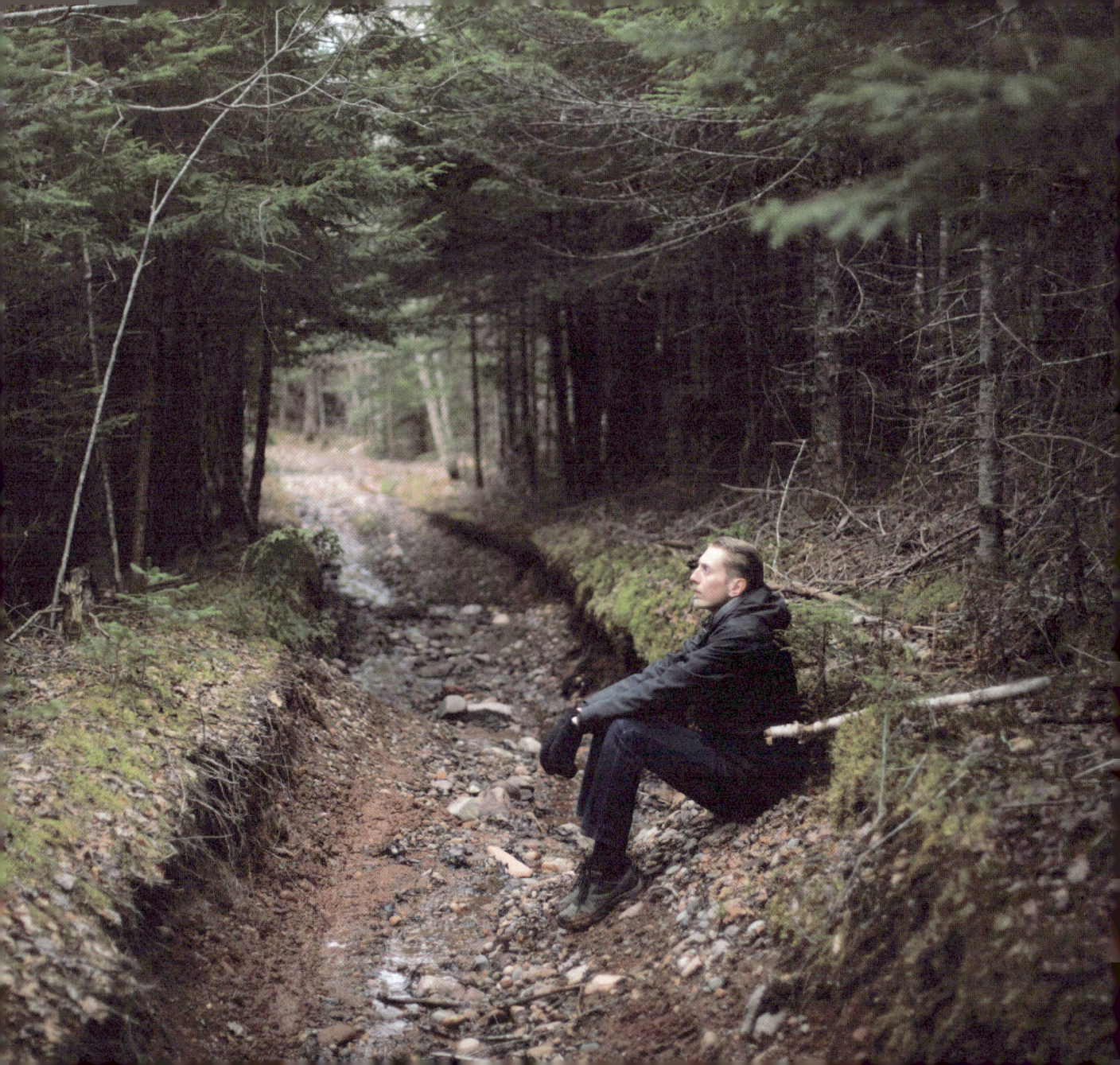

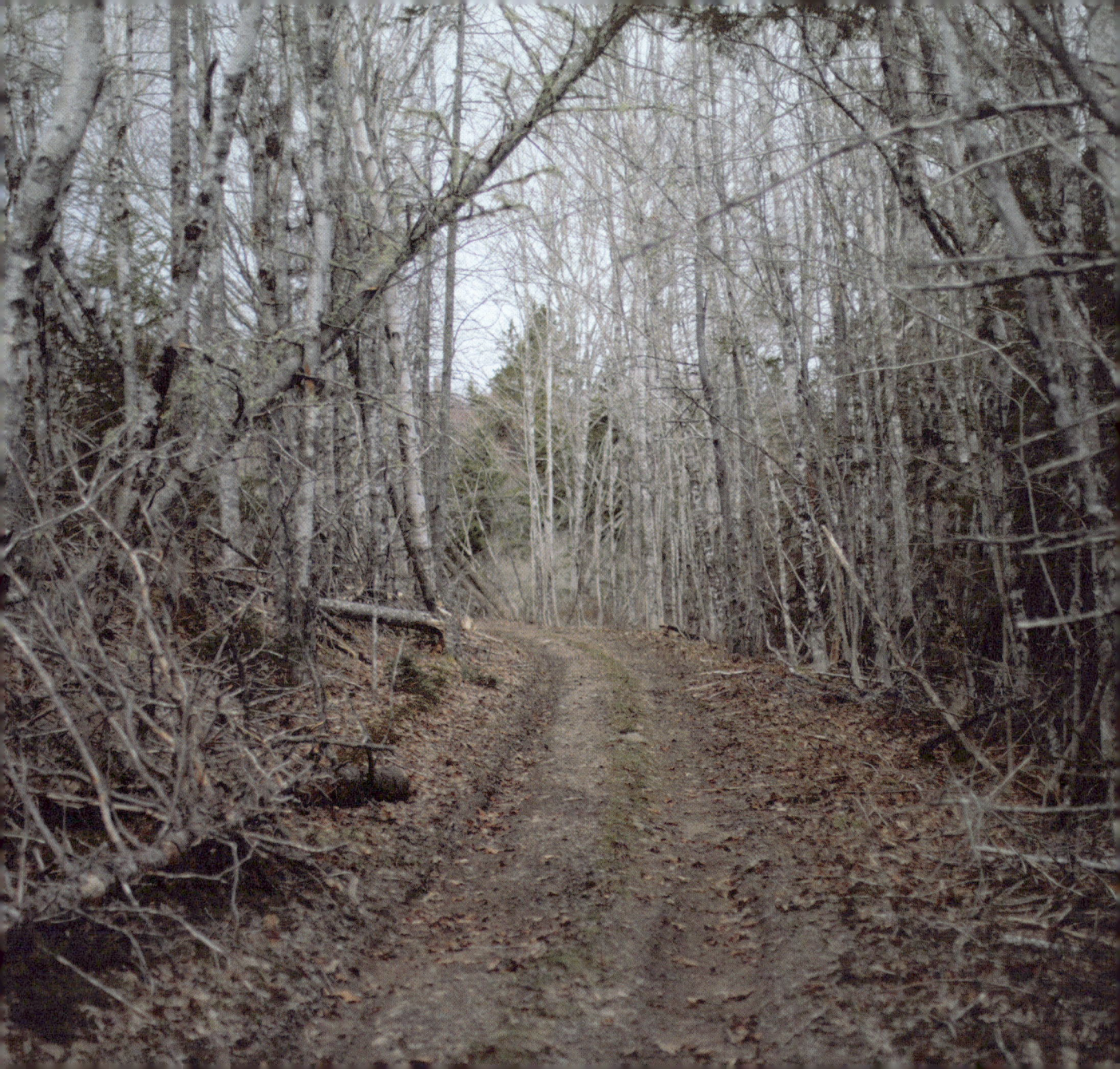

OLD SAINT JOSEPH'S ROAD

St. Joseph, Antigonish County

The secretive spaces west of Ohio River are scattered with human signs, hints of who once lived here. Settled in centuries past, when that body of water was still known by the unwieldy name West River of Antigonish. These woods were cleared and homesteads settled by folks like Donald McDonald, John McMillan, and Murdoch McRae. This tumble-down hole in the earth is all that remains of the McMillan cellar walls, a few stacked rocks scattered among the self-destructive deadfall. But his fields haven't gone to waste, still hayed to this day down to the shores of St. Josephs Lake. I spent an hour breaking back and tossing out the fallen branches, kicking around the rusty cans and bottles, and thinking about everything this foundation no longer holds up.

This was never the way to get anywhere else. Frequented only by the folks who took it to and from home and never thought to be crossed by the likes of strangers like me. Ending up accidentally down the depths of Old Saint Joseph's Road—it's an unlikely occurrence even now. Through twisting turns and sleepless hollows, with hearts that follow where feet lead. Spring seemed like a distant promise this morning, cutting back and forth from scattered showers to flurries. Bits of green grass were all that gave it away for good. Cold wind pulled a chill straight through me, a welcoming kind of rhythm as

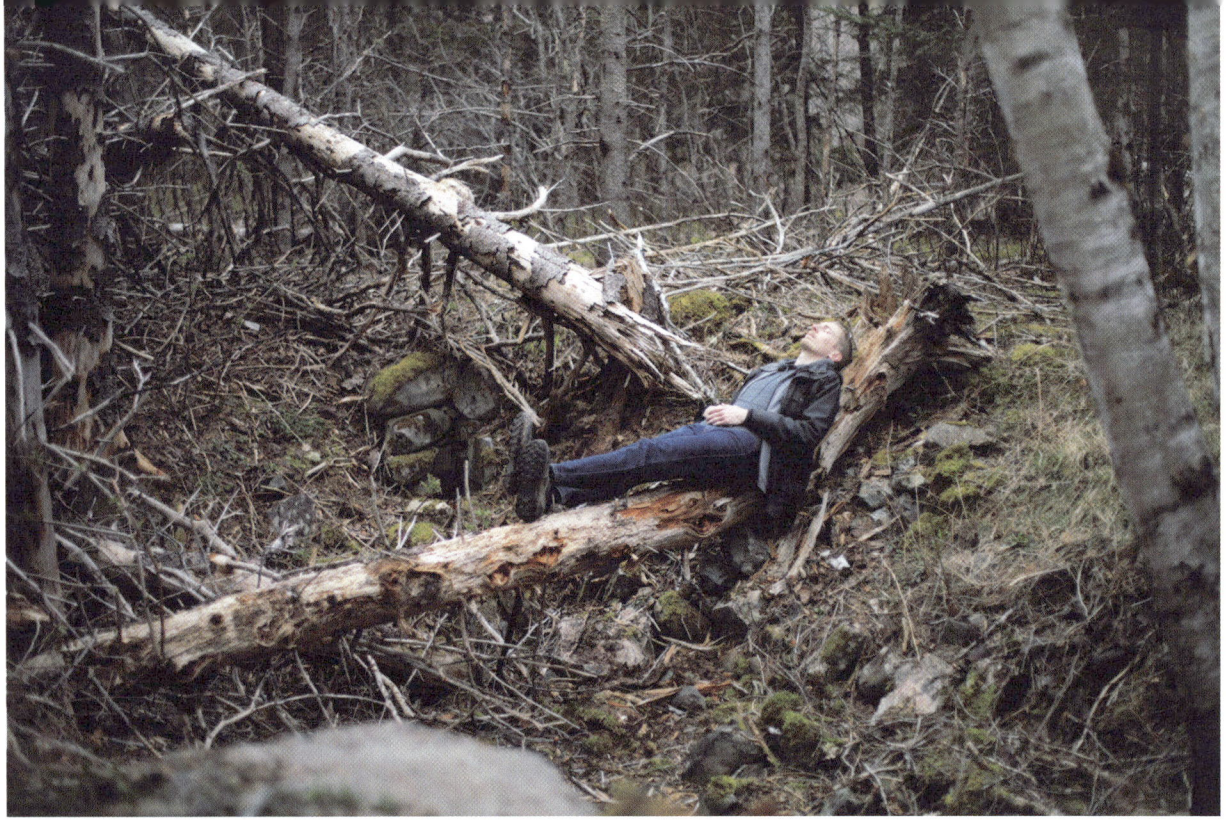

I walked where old souls turned to bones. Why not put down roots?

That rusty truck body (a mid-40s Chevrolet) was pushed off the edge of the field above and left to last on the shores of a trickling, nameless brook. Where it fell from was owned at various times by Donald, Nancy, and Mary McDonald, and Catherine Gohan.

It's more than likely that one of their family name once sat behind this wheel as driver. Every old farmstead left something similar behind. In the days before wreckers, hauling off to the junkyard was an extra, unnecessary expense. So, you stripped what you could for parts, then dragged the corpse the shortest possible distance out of view—usually to the

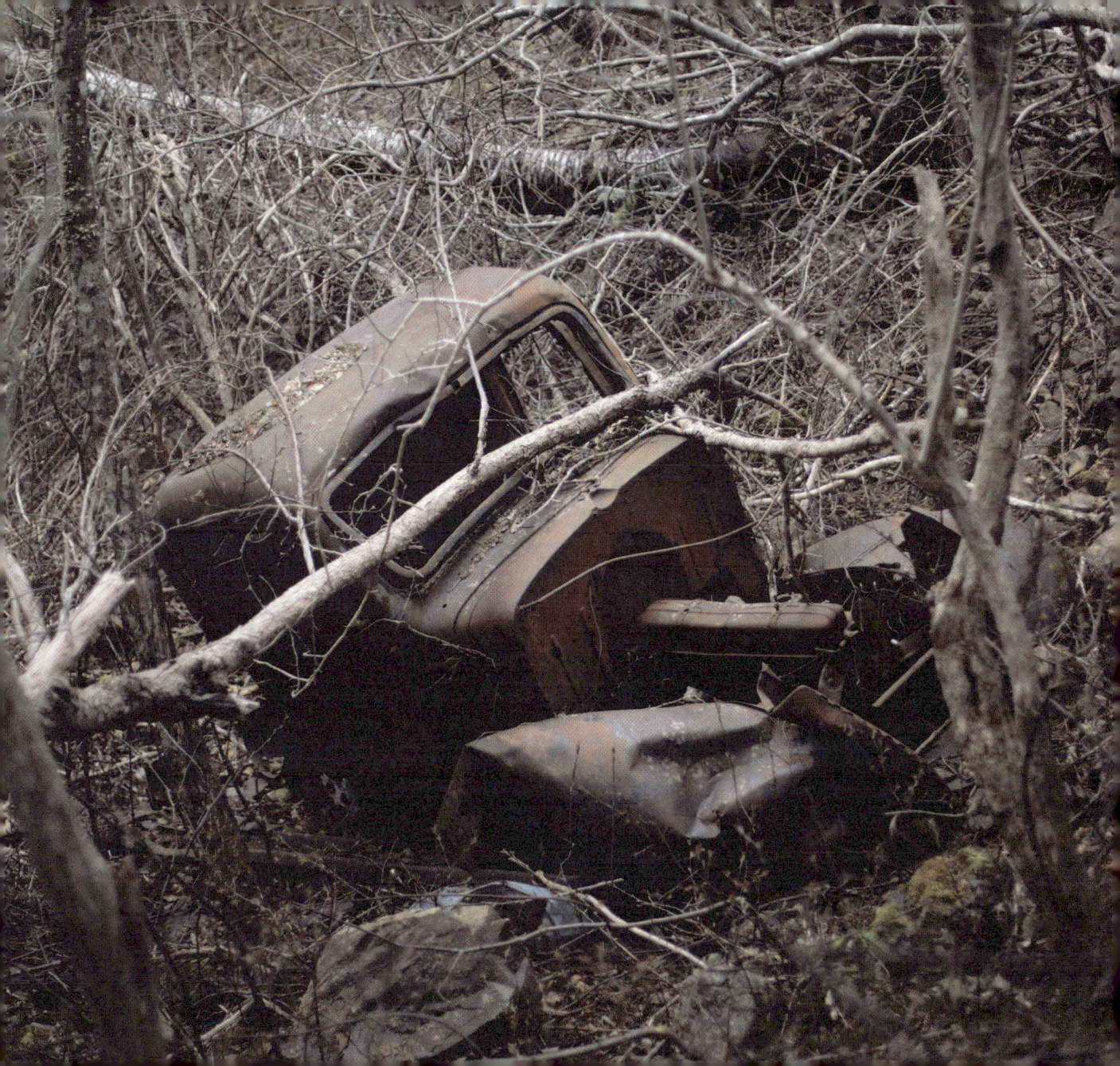

corners of the property. Everything gets so shrouded out here in young-growth country. I missed the sight on my hike south on Old Saint Joseph's Road and barely spotted it on the return back north. If it'd been summer, I wouldn't have had a hope. Lost in the mist of a billion shades of brown. It's hard to believe in that sea of green soon coming.

45.54144, -62.09064

2.9 kilometres. Runs south from Saint Joseph's Road, down to where maintenance resumes at the driveway for Civic #89. Park at the mouth of the road on the shoulder.

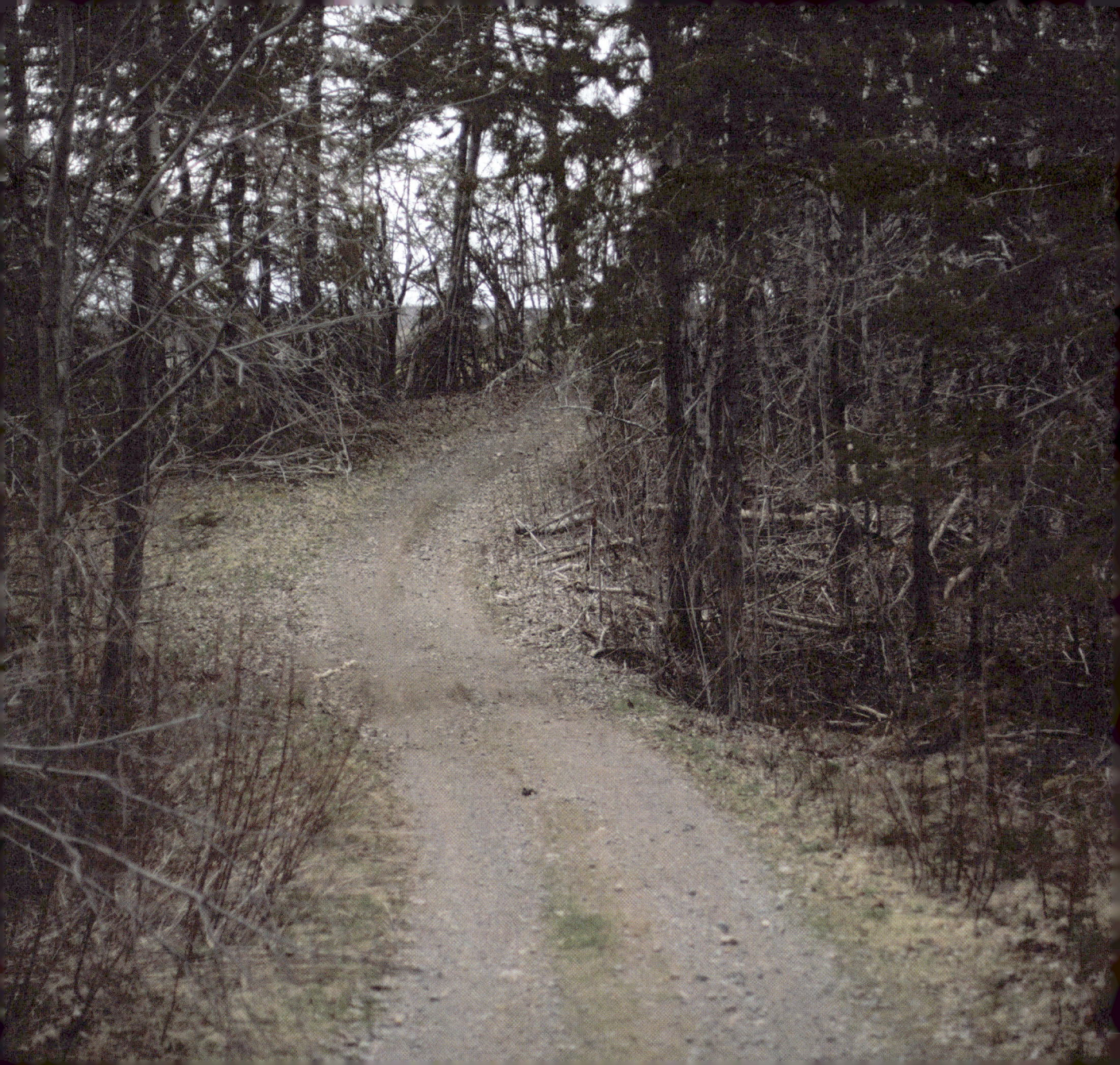

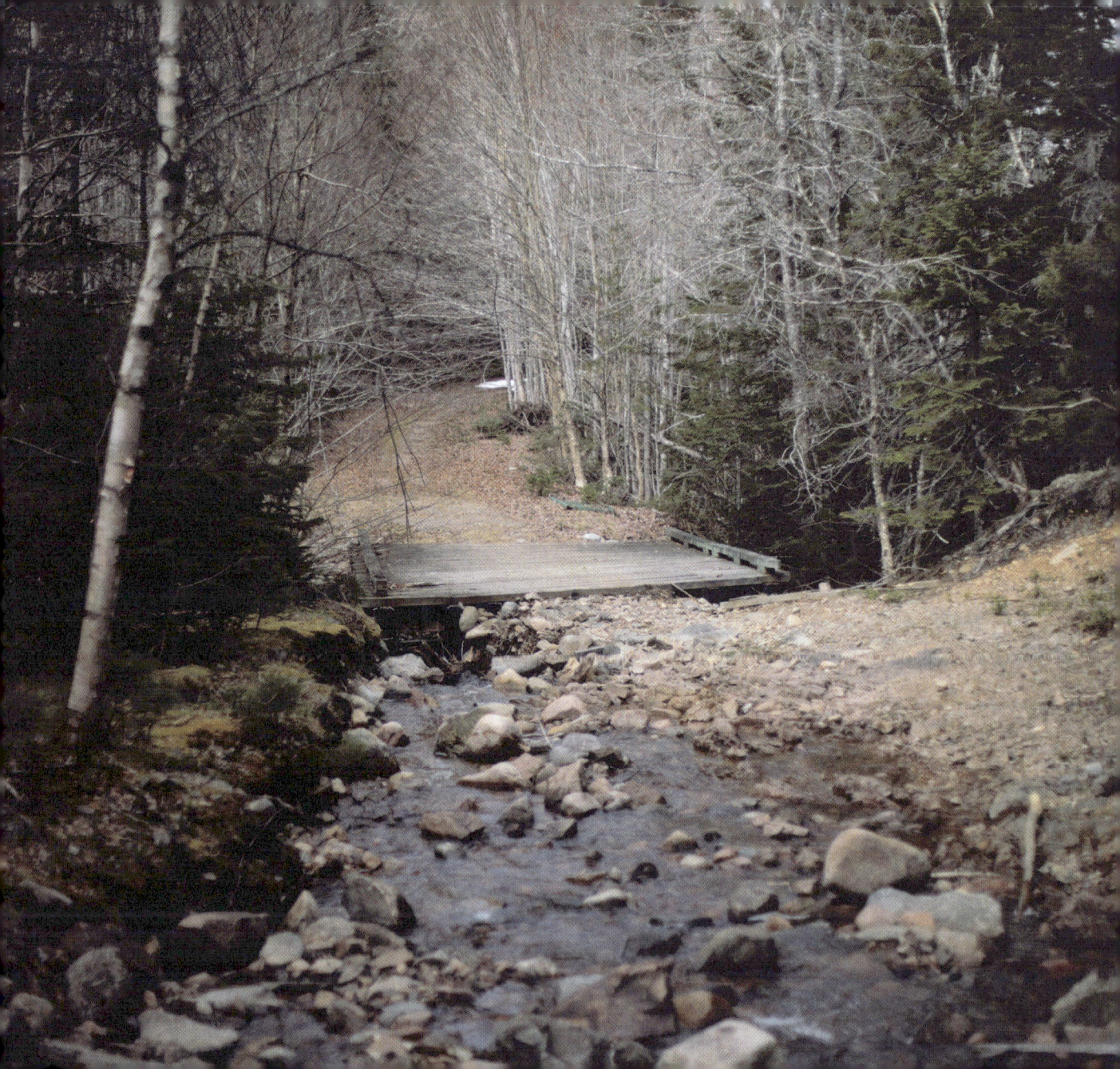

KELLYS LANE

Englishtown, Victoria County

When we were kids, we used to say: "The first of May is barefoot day." Don't know where that came from, but it always seemed to send us running through the muddy backyard with cold toes. Today finds me a good six weeks after the start of spring, but deep and dark places still linger with the final bits of snow, spaces in shade from dawn till dusk. What a funny feeling thinking that these last patches could almost be shrouded by leaf cover. No—they still should be melted in just enough time. As I made my way through the eastern woods of Cape Breton, I was sensing that old lonely feeling of being as far from home as I can be, while still in my homeland. Nova Scotia can seem like such a terribly vast place when you really get exploring. I feel unfamiliar in so many quarters of a province where I've belonged all my life.

Kellys Mountain really called me out this morning. I was awake far earlier than I'd typically be, ready to make the most of my limited time away. Winding up and up on a slow and twisting climb, with no clear view of the cove far below, I got the vaguest sense of gravity dragging. It's a sensation that I can only describe as drifting upwards. Like a balloon filled with only just enough helium to break these bonds, I made my circling ascent into the sleepy upper depths. It wasn't long before cold shook loose and body heat took hold. I started carrying my coat and feeling the warmth accumulated by nothing but

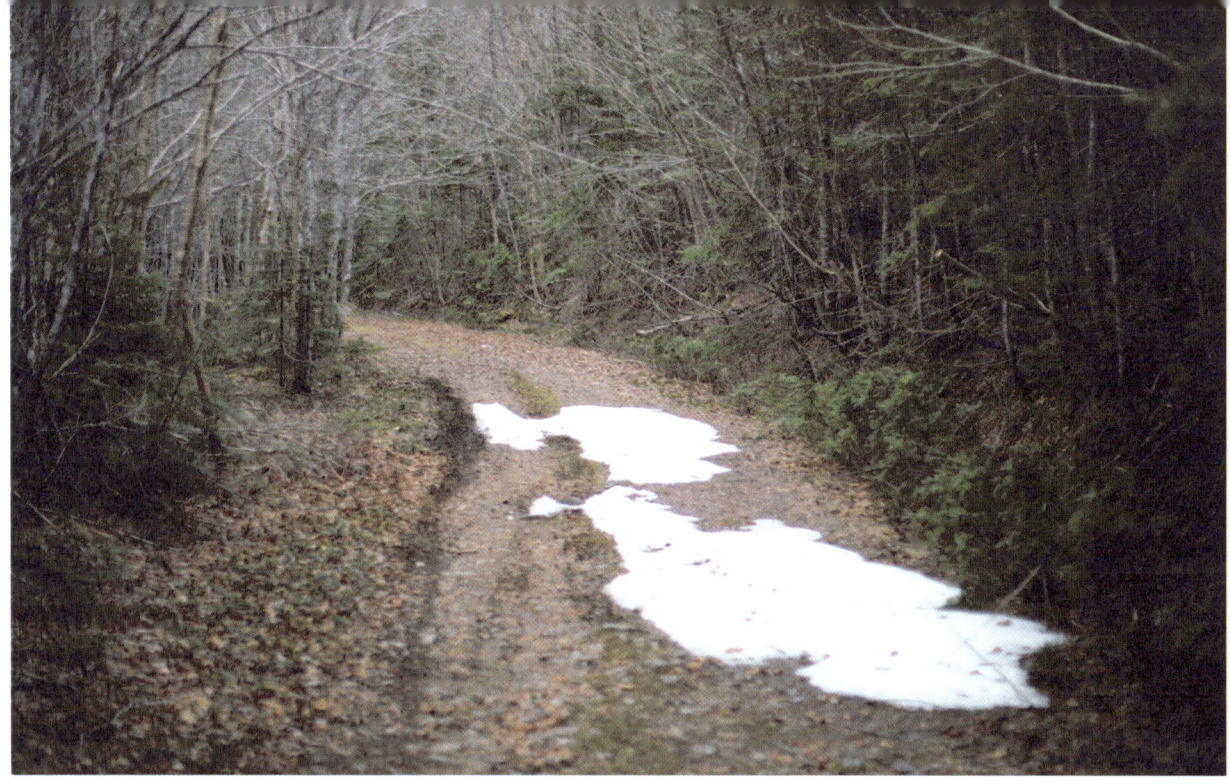

lifted legs and pounding heart. In the early years, this road marked the backcountry border for the families Cann, Kerr, McAulay, McLeod, Montgomery, and Sellon. Their way through the woods to where the mass of Crown land country held sway. It's still that story today—deep and wild as you like it.

Kellys Lane has become confused between the ruts and watercourses. If every derelict track has a heart and soul, this road could certainly claim Sallys Brook. You spot her namesake not long past the last home, running deep down in the hollow on your left. Then, the first bridge unveils itself, a well-built beast that's been steadily eroded on both sides. It seems it'll soon be an island to itself, waiting on an eventual toppling. About another half-kilometre uphill, the stream is spanned once again by a much more

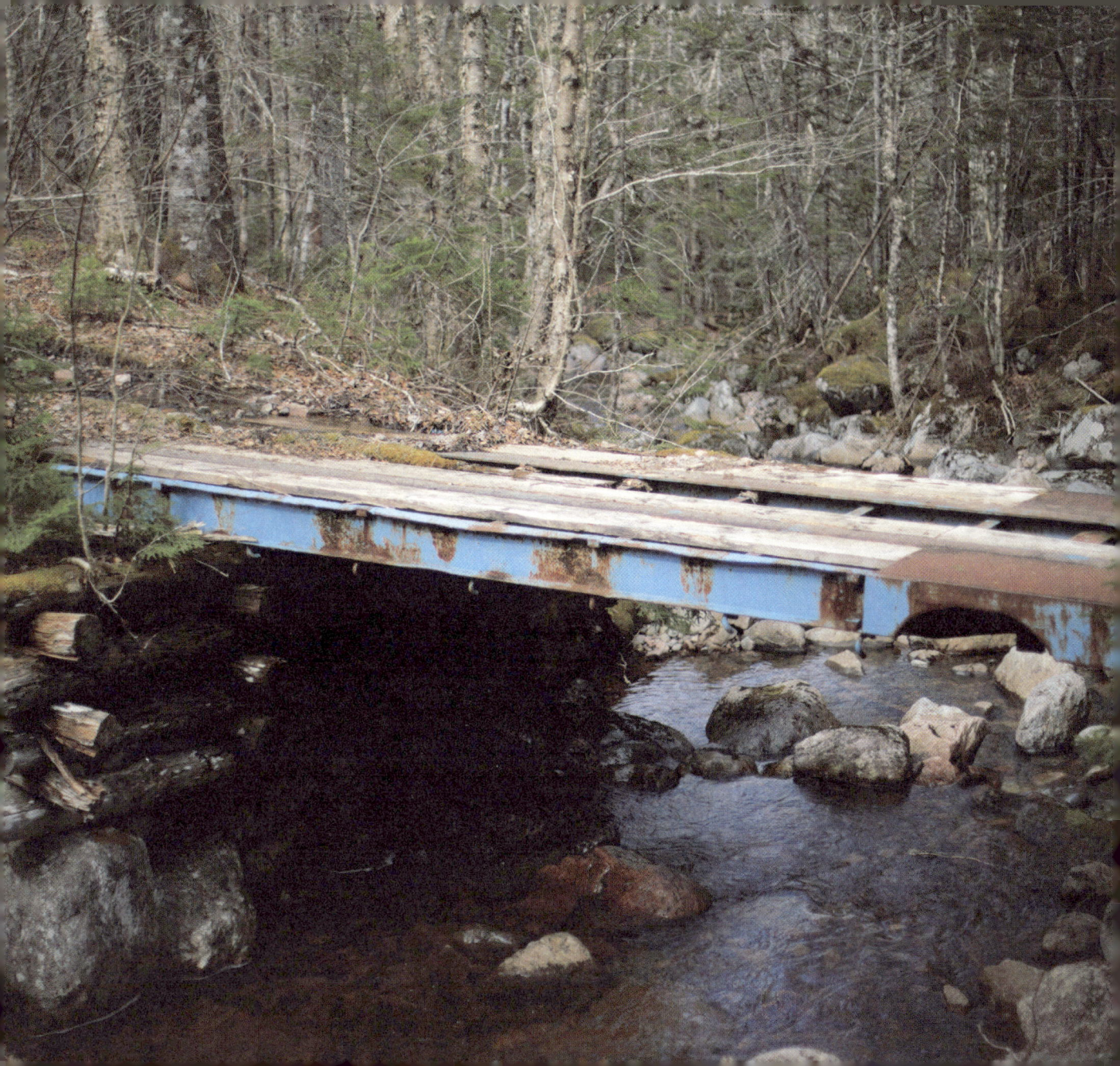

humble, precarious crossing. Rusty metal mounted on rotting timbers, fighting back a downfall. I feel an almost endless fascination for what nature can do to our infrastructure left alone. The devices of water and gravity, corrosion and rot eating away at everything not set in stone. If we were the sort to build bridges from rocks, perhaps they'd last a little longer without us. But maybe we're better off with the mortal reminder.

46.27981, -60.52909

3.8 kilometres. Runs south from the driveway of Civic #373 on Kellys Lane, crossing Sallys Brook twice and climbing over the mountain until regular logging resumes. Park on the shoulder.

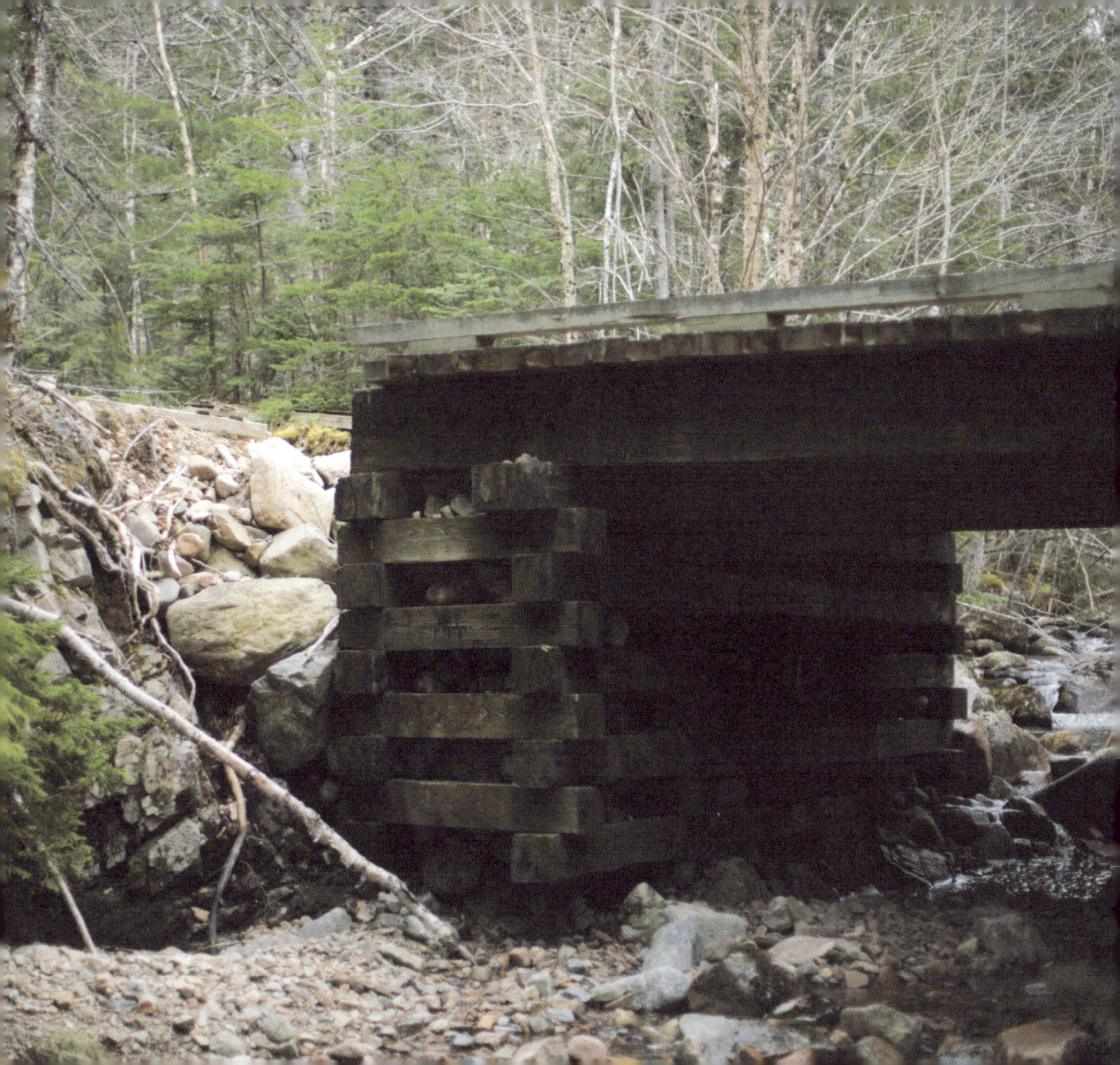

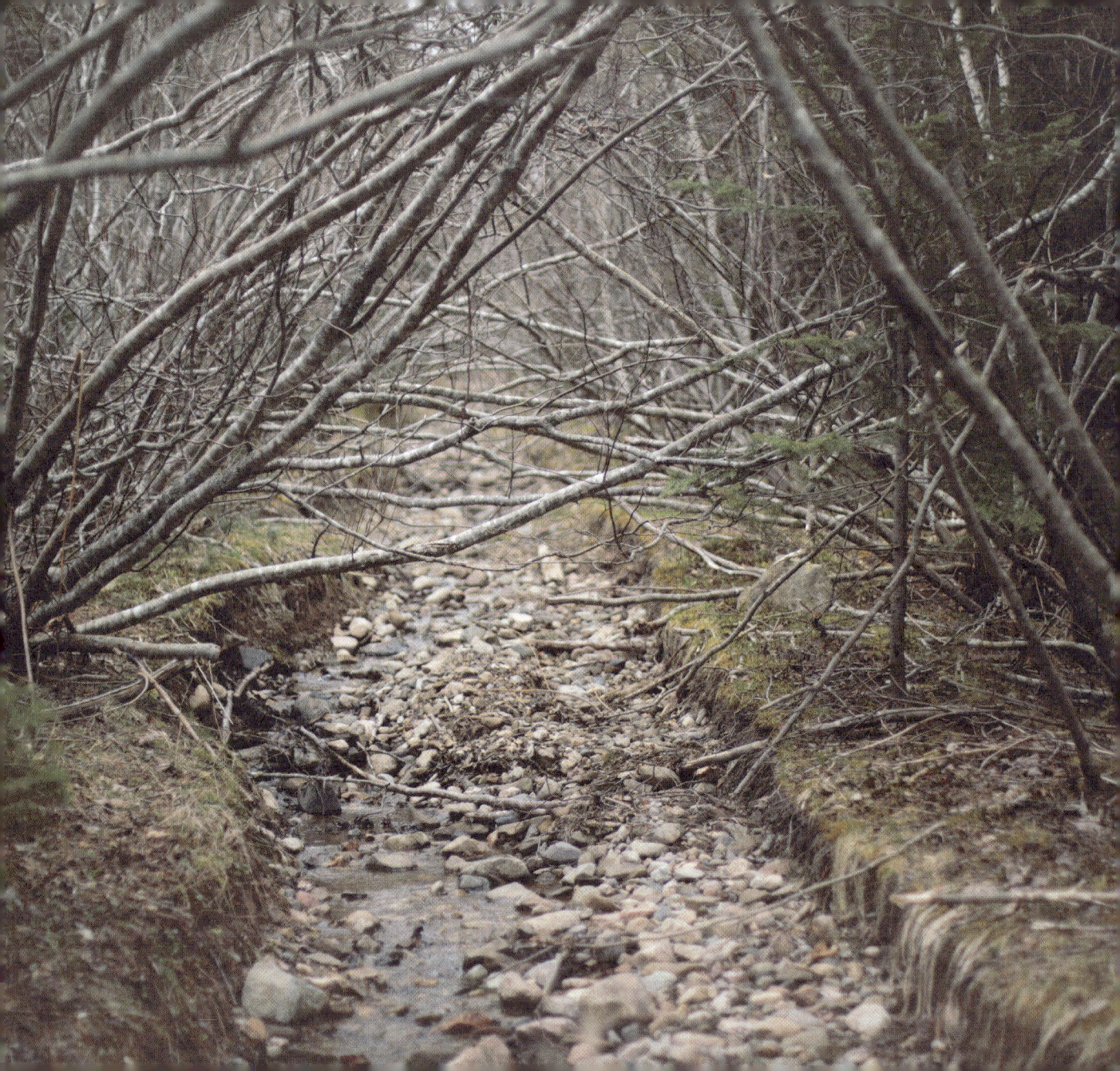

MACINTYRE ROAD

Scotch Lake, Cape Breton County

When it comes to hours of tripping, ducking, and dodging, sometimes I've had enough. But what happens when you keep going is a feeling worth chasing. There's a deep satisfaction when those ends finally meet, dotted lines through spaces that society forgot. There's no compulsion like when it's going, going, but not quite gone just yet. MacIntyre Road really tested me, but I broke through the blank space on the map—and that's a high few things can match. When every joint seems to find a new way to ache, and I learn to appreciate even the smallest break through the brush. Squirming through the branches, startling hares who are surprised that anything my size would be there. I upset a fair few birds, as well.

Above the trail, behind the brush, I caught sight of a small and rocky overhang. Just enough to take shelter from a storm, if you were so desperate or inclined. I've got no intention of spending the night out here, but I heartily recommend going feral for at least a few hours at a time. There's no doubt it'll do you good.

You could say that some roads are more trouble than they're worth to hike. But I'm tempted by tracks left to their worst estimation, abandoned long ago to what water and wilderness can do. MacIntyre Road runs through some pretty tangled forest from Scotch Lake down to Leitches Creek, and past the mostly unsettled shores of Roach Lake. These woods

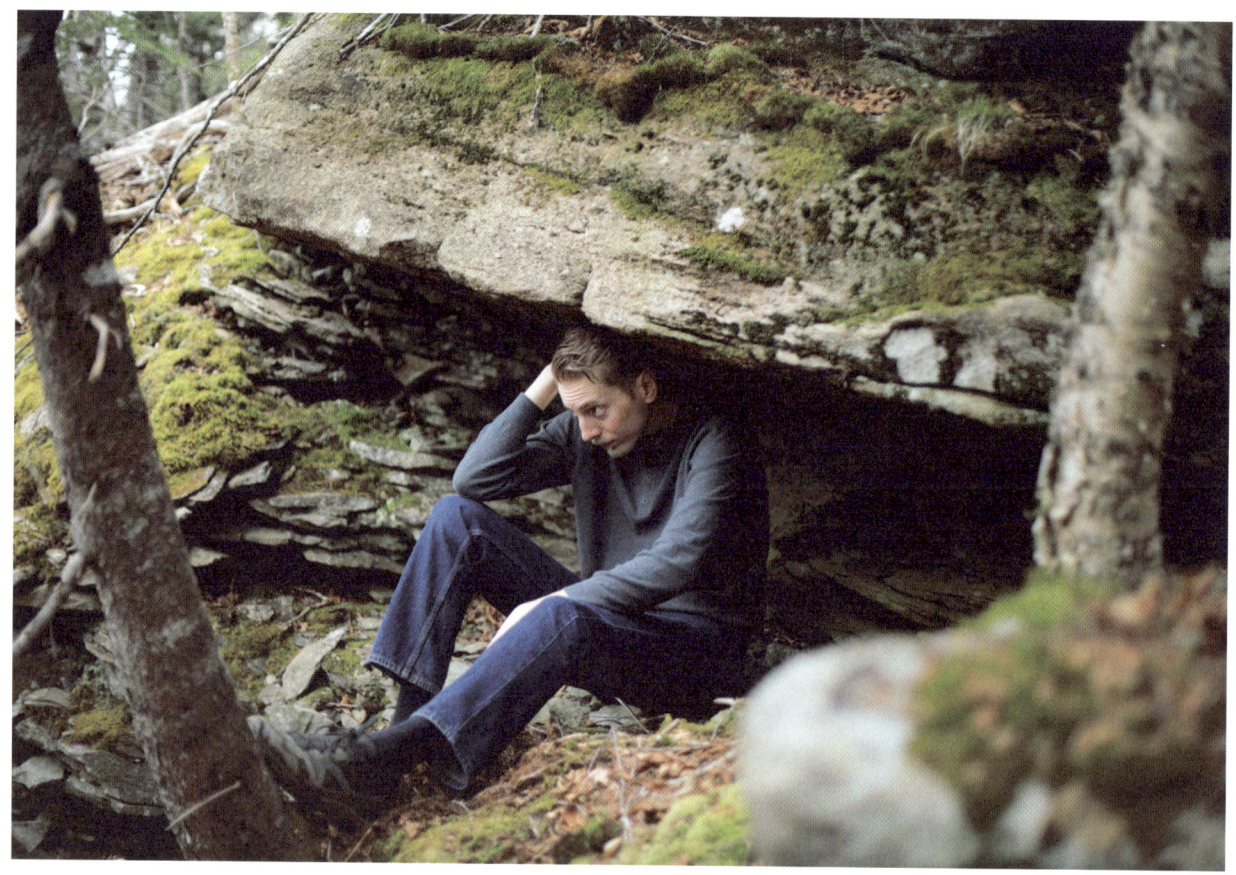

were never much inhabited, more the concern of local loggers—though Effie Ferguson and John McCormack did live in some of the deepest portions. If they left signs of settlement, well, it seems they've long gone away. But the road they took to escape to (or from) civilization remains. Against the advice of my wearing body, this was my second aching adventure of the day. I'd spent the morning in high

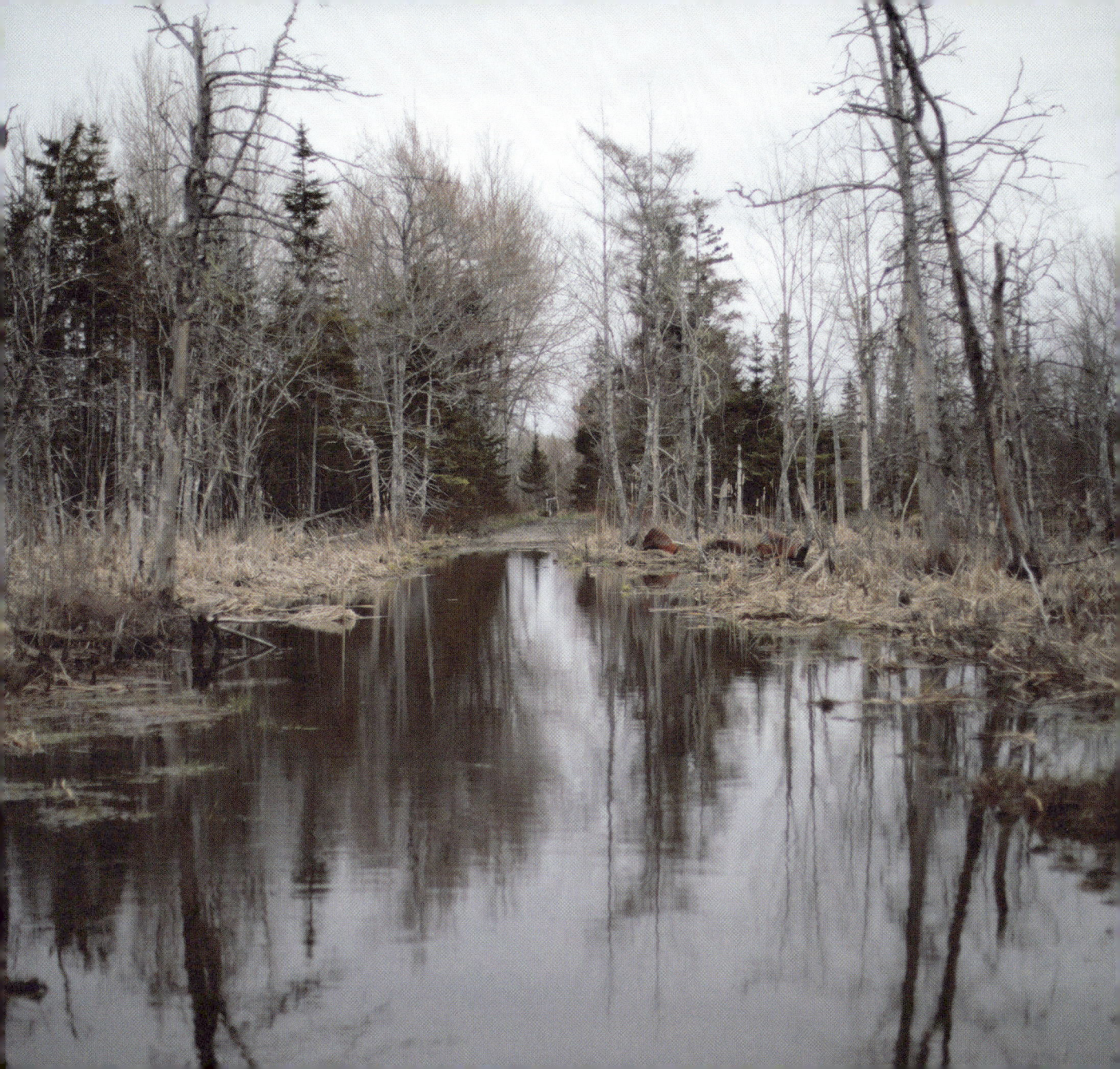

country and then a long afternoon in these rocky lowlands. Things started getting a little swampy, and I spotted the scattered blackflies buzzing circles around my skull. I counted myself lucky that it was cool enough to keep them tame. I'd be mighty unhappy in a place like this just two weeks later, the particular hell of late spring Nova Scotia, when everything begs for blood.

46.17580, -60.36487

3.7 kilometres. Runs southeast past Civic #159 and down to Leitches Creek Road. Park at the turnaround spot.

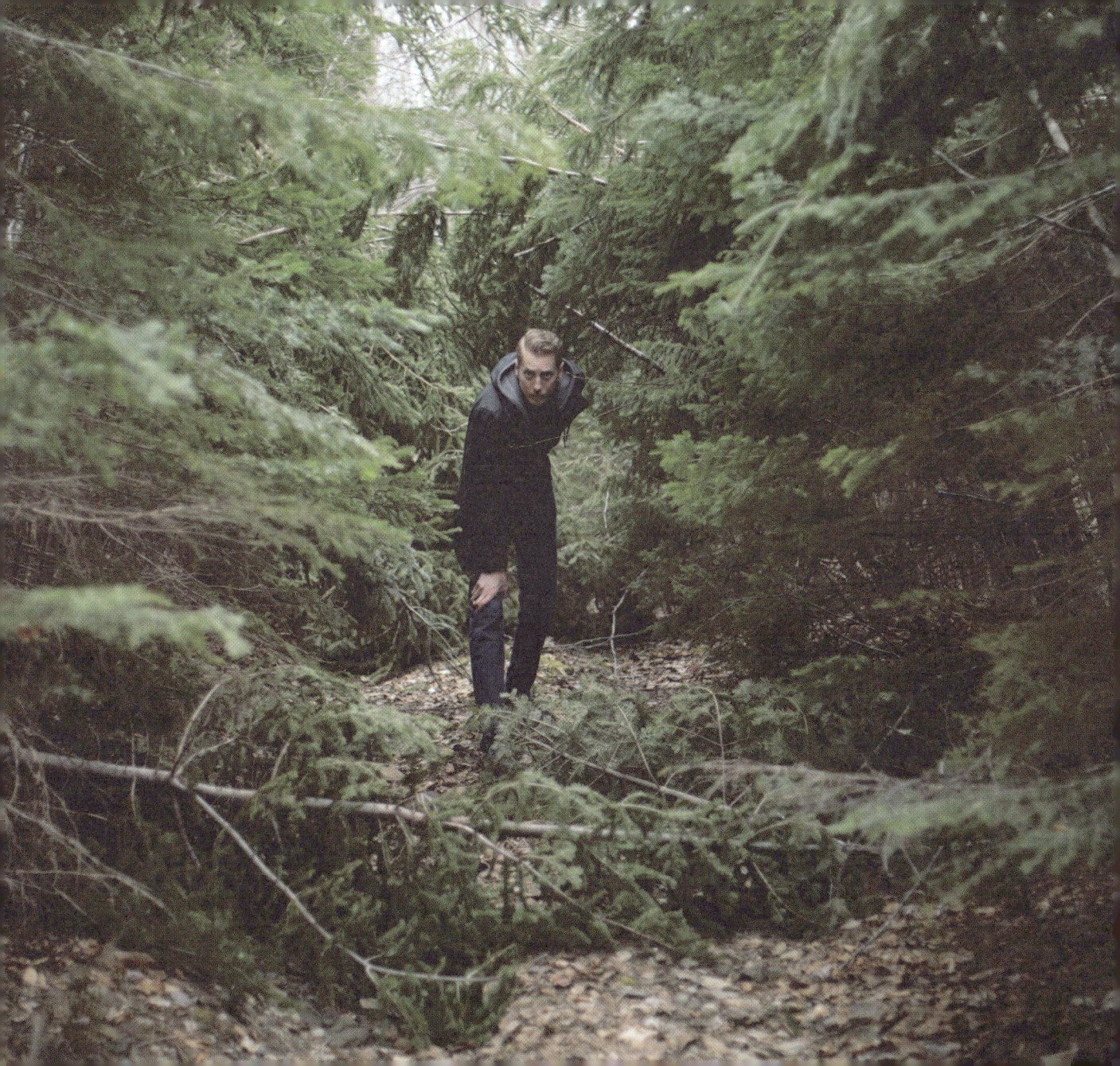

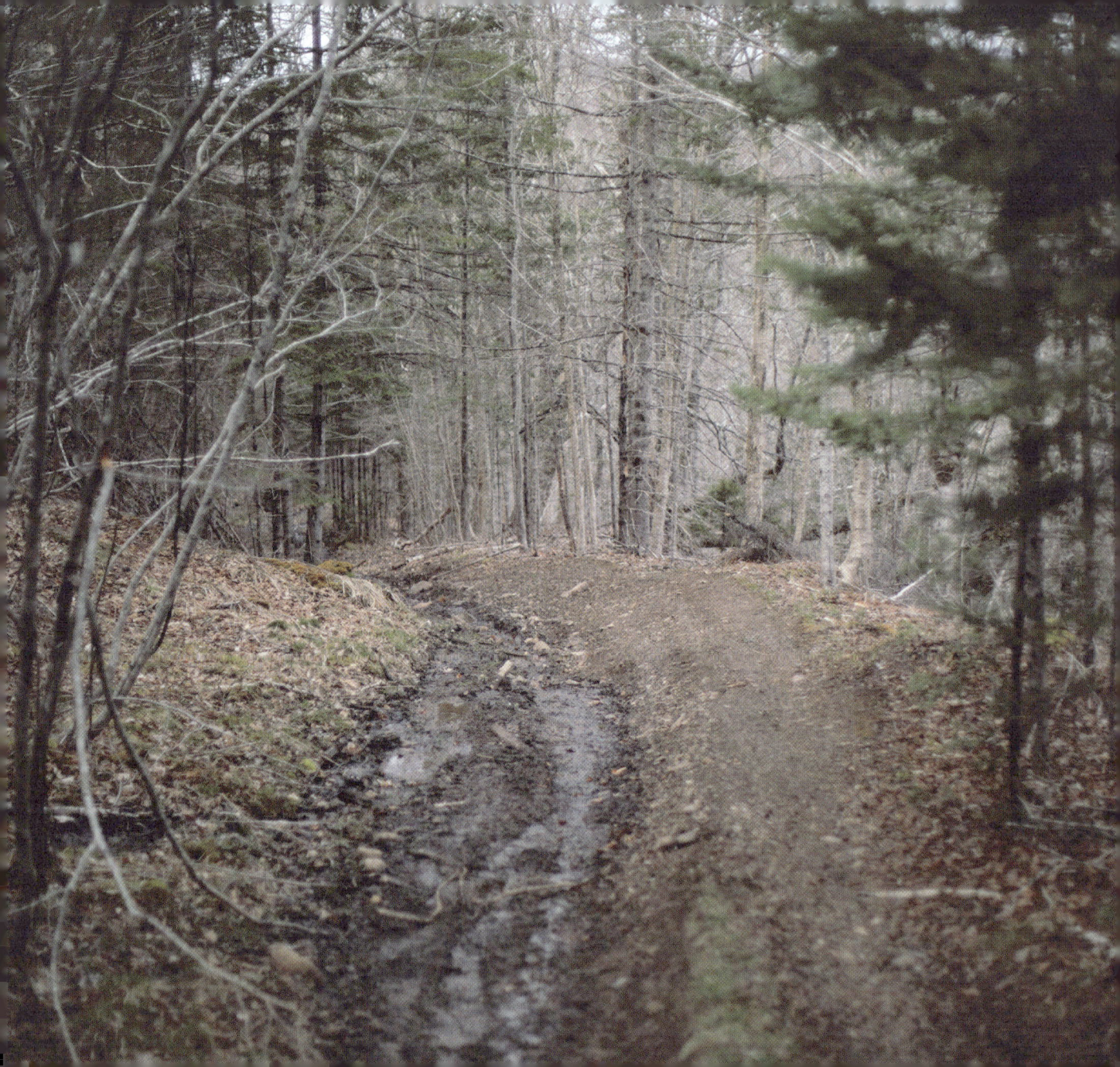

EAST FOLLY MOUNTAIN ROAD

Folly Mountain, Colchester County

Earlier in the afternoon, I was down the coast for a hike that proved fruitless, on an abandoned road that soon became obliterated by clear-cuts and brush. This forgotten crossing over Folly River was my second option, and it was a last-minute arrival, stumbling in on the edge of evening. I parked nearby at a cemetery and walked down from the roadside, quickly dropping as the bottom fell out. A steep descent into a pristine hollow never fails to spark my sense of wonder. It hides everything from sight, keeps the outside at bay. Trickling water to hide the white noise of traffic, high hills to block the light—and the ghost of a bridge with only concrete abutments left to tell the tale. The last vehicle to drive above this sleepy body of water was in the 90s, when the crumbling span was finally surrendered forever. One side fallen in the water and the other soon to follow, or maybe that final upheaval will take longer than you'd think. Caught up in a crumbling past.

Short sections like these hold no great value to the long-distance hiker, but keeping them as public right of ways is deeply essential for folks who just want to escape a while. Up by the pavement, someone has strung an illegal chain across the entrance

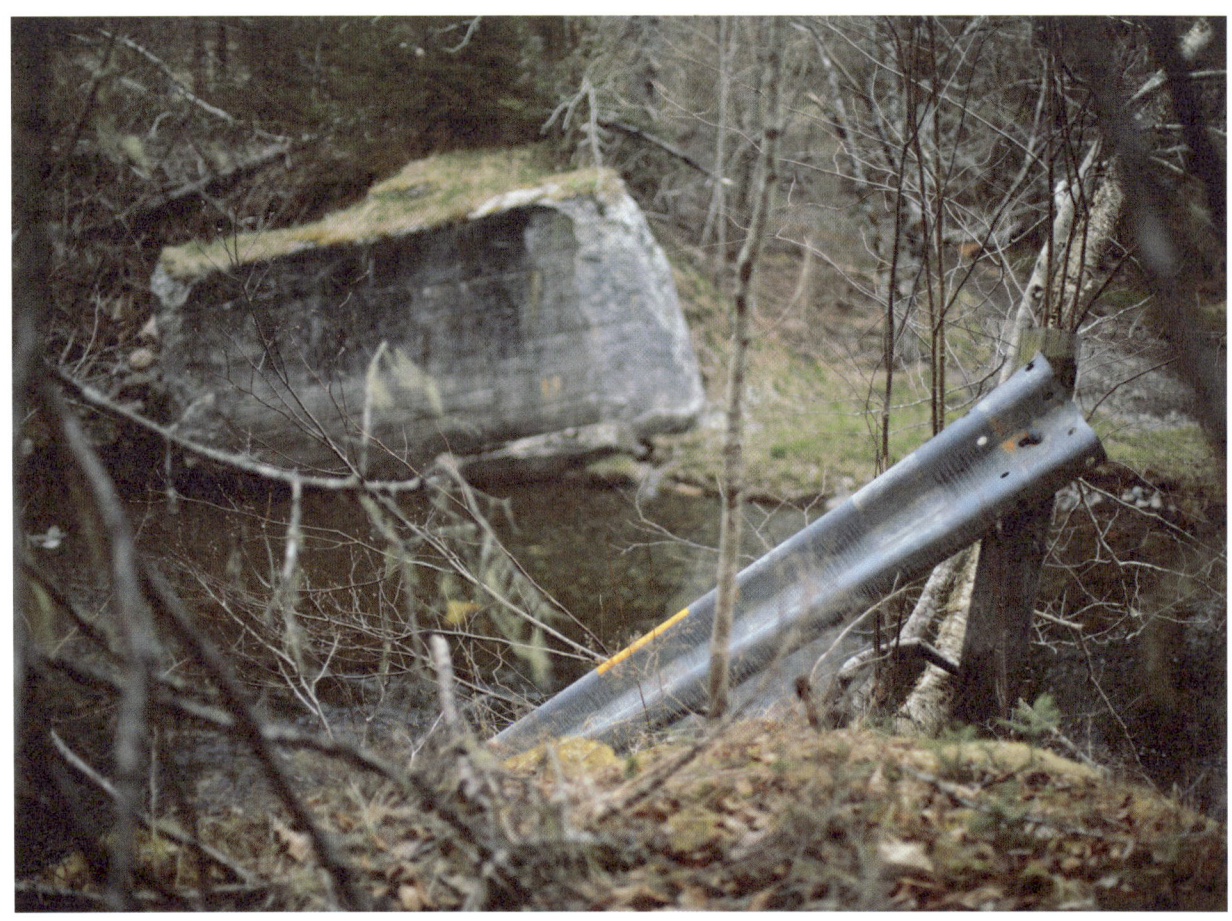

in an attempt to claim it as their own. That's a familiar arrogance you can commonly find in the countryside, a belief that pretending something is yours is enough to win it out. Blockaders; keepers, if you will. But it was our great-great-grandparents who cut this path that opened it up for all to use,

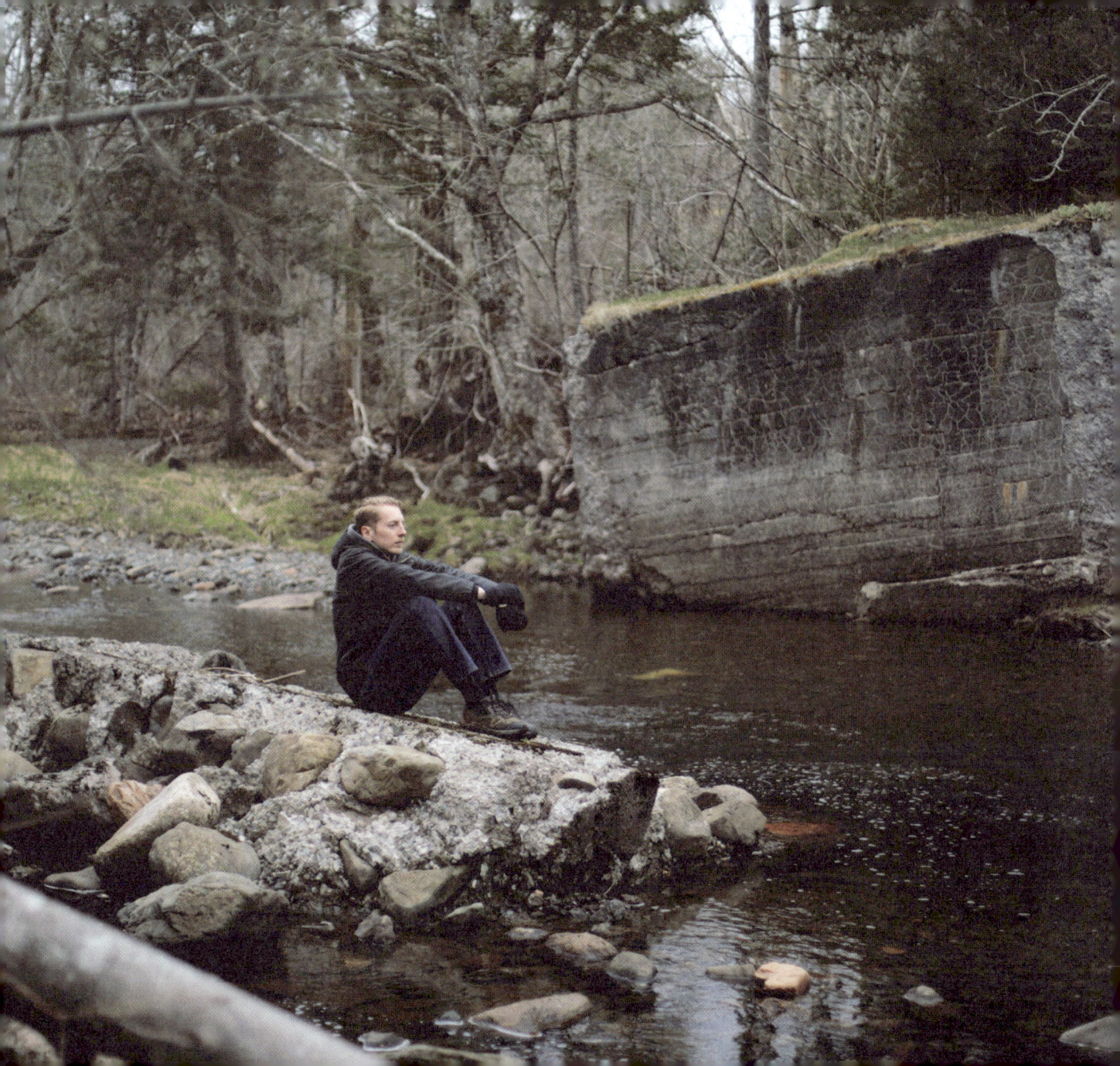

and later government agencies that kept it main-tained for generations after. In its abandonment, the western end of East Folly Mountain Road has been entrusted to wanderers like me, following ruts to places the past has swallowed whole. Think of it as an out-of-civilization experience. Always worth the rapture.

45.47824, -63.52841

480 metres. Runs northeast across from Civic #1700 on Highway 4, down to a former bridge crossing of Folly River. Park just north, at Folly Mountain Cemetery.

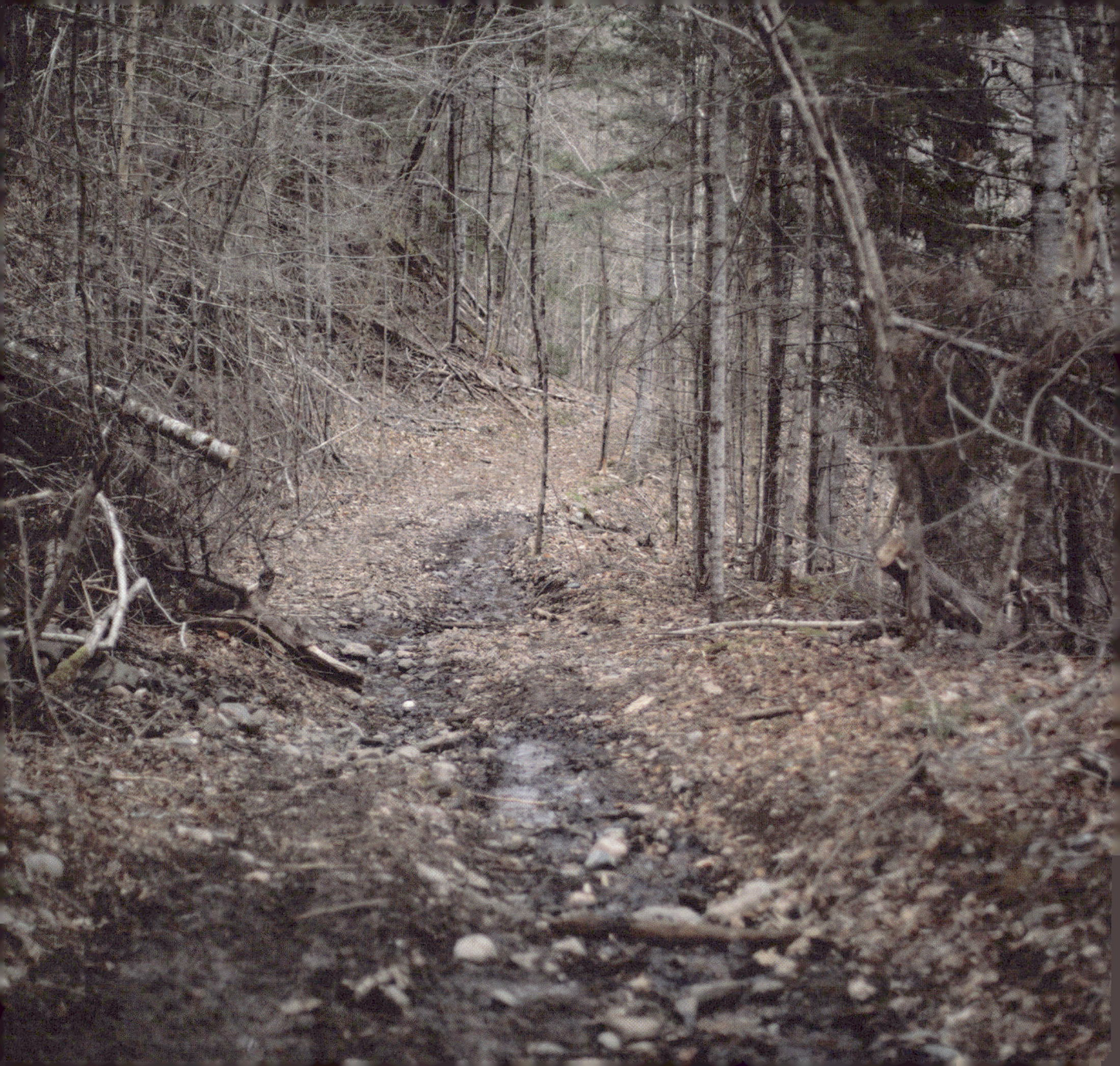

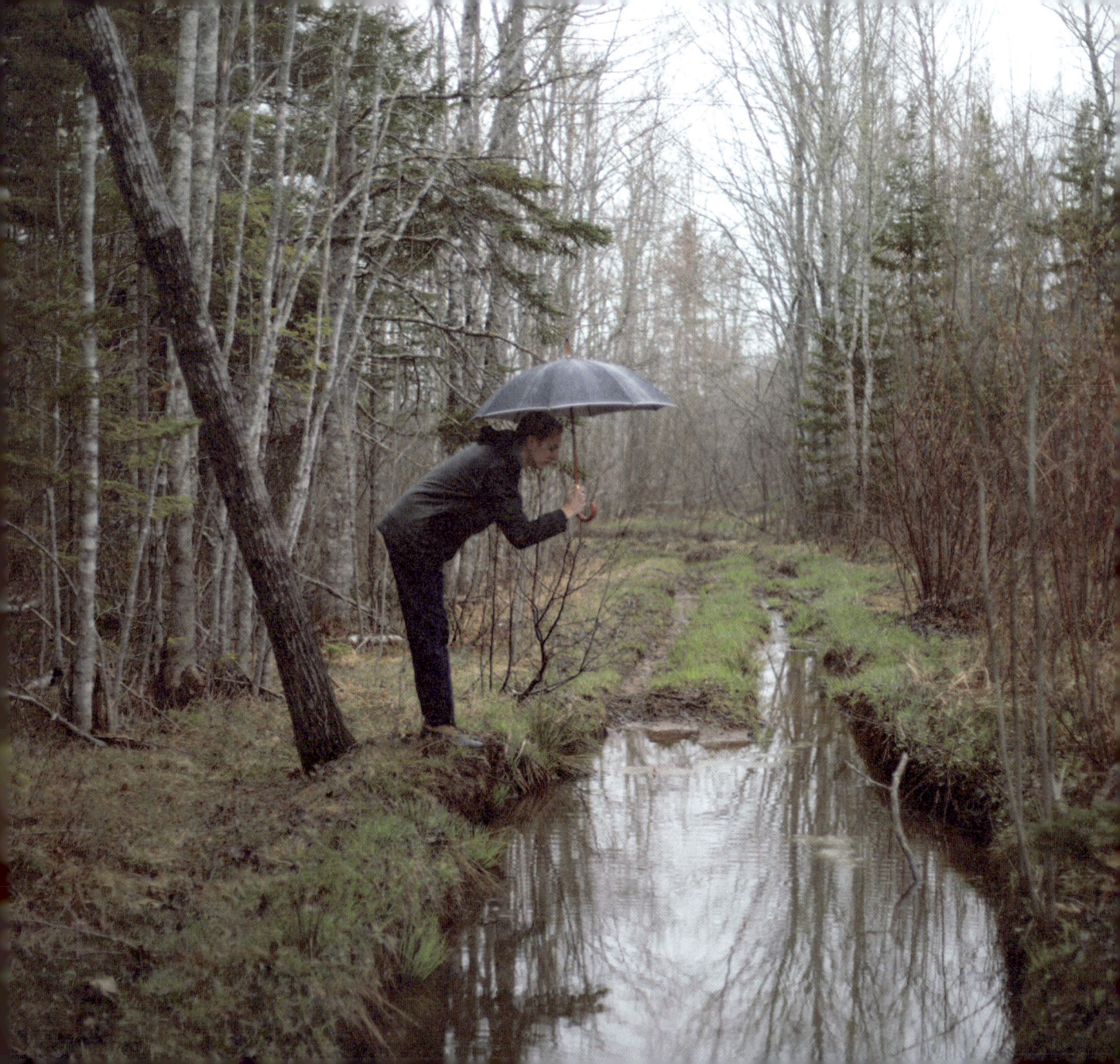

COACH ROAD

Upper Falmouth, Hants County

There was a time when Coach Road really mattered. Back in the day, before bridges spanned the widest points of the Avon and Gaspereau Rivers, this was part of your inland highway connecting Windsor and Wolfville. It was quite an undertaking, and still shows results for the effort. The first section out of Sangster Bridge Road is mostly level, which turns out to be a bad thing. Things start going wrong in a rush. Water settles in a marshy bog that you'll be leaping over and slipping through. Fertile ground for getting mired, and a good reminder why I'm always on foot. I'd rather duck a fallen tree or skirt a road-wide puddle than get stopped in my tracks and tires. I'll leave the winches and chainsaws for the more motorized among us. I like to travel light and burn the fuel of my muscle and blood. The road bottoms out at Allen Brook, a peaceful kind of liquid intersection. The rest is cut wider through the woods, mostly high and dry for the final two-thirds through. It's a long and languid hill to summit, slow climb and fall on both sides. When you're hiking up from either direction, it feels like you'll never get there.

I left a few deep breaths on the shoulder, chasing down the long way home. It's clear I'm not the toughest hiker, but after all the distance covered, I'm certain I've got endurance on my side. The full span of this hike is five and a half kilometres of rock and mud, none of which I'd dare my car to cover. The

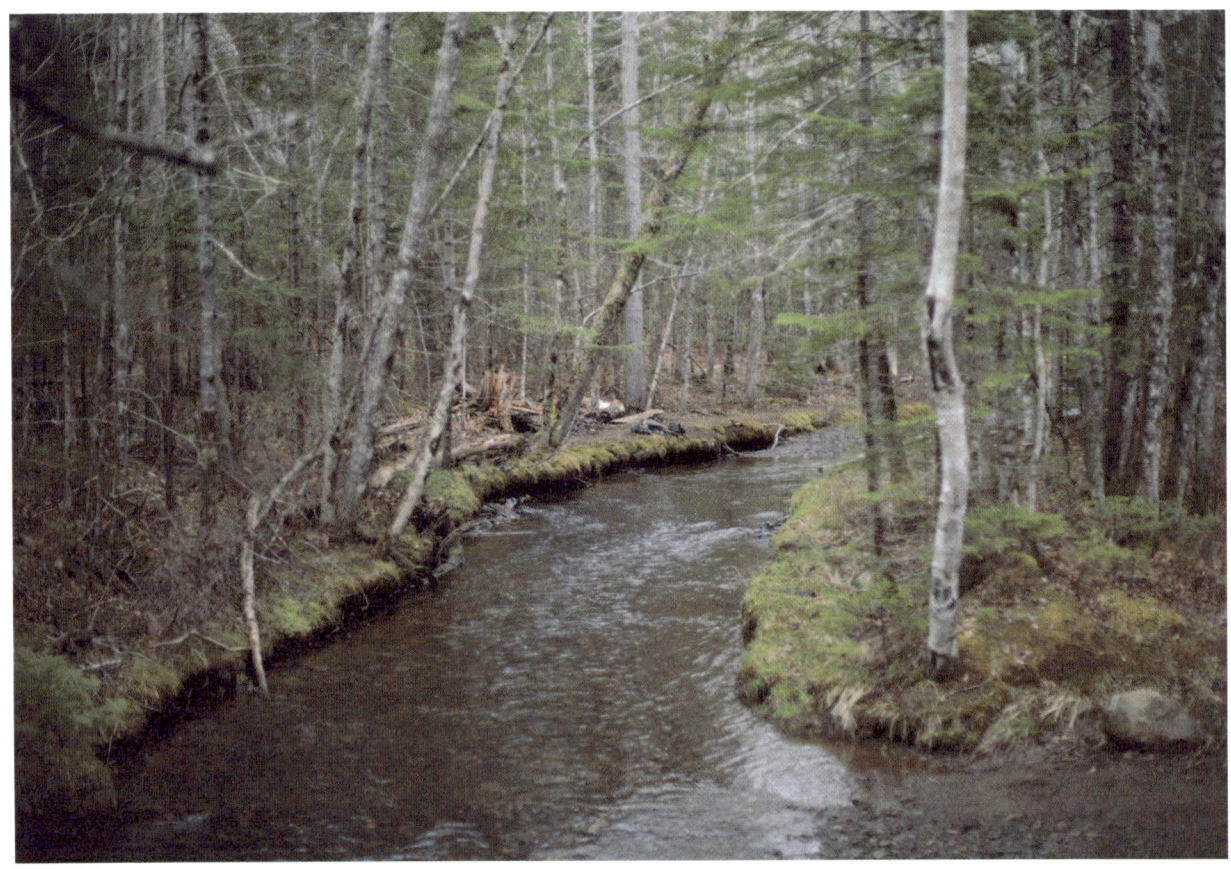

long way out doesn't feel half as hard as the return, eleven kilometres when it's all been said and seen. I sense every step by the end, my body's reminder that I'm never so tough as I intend. Some of us have this notion that there's only one kind of adventure—the sort you can brag about. Mountain climbing or week-long hikes, massive efforts matched with your fair share of suffering. But I believe that being an explorer

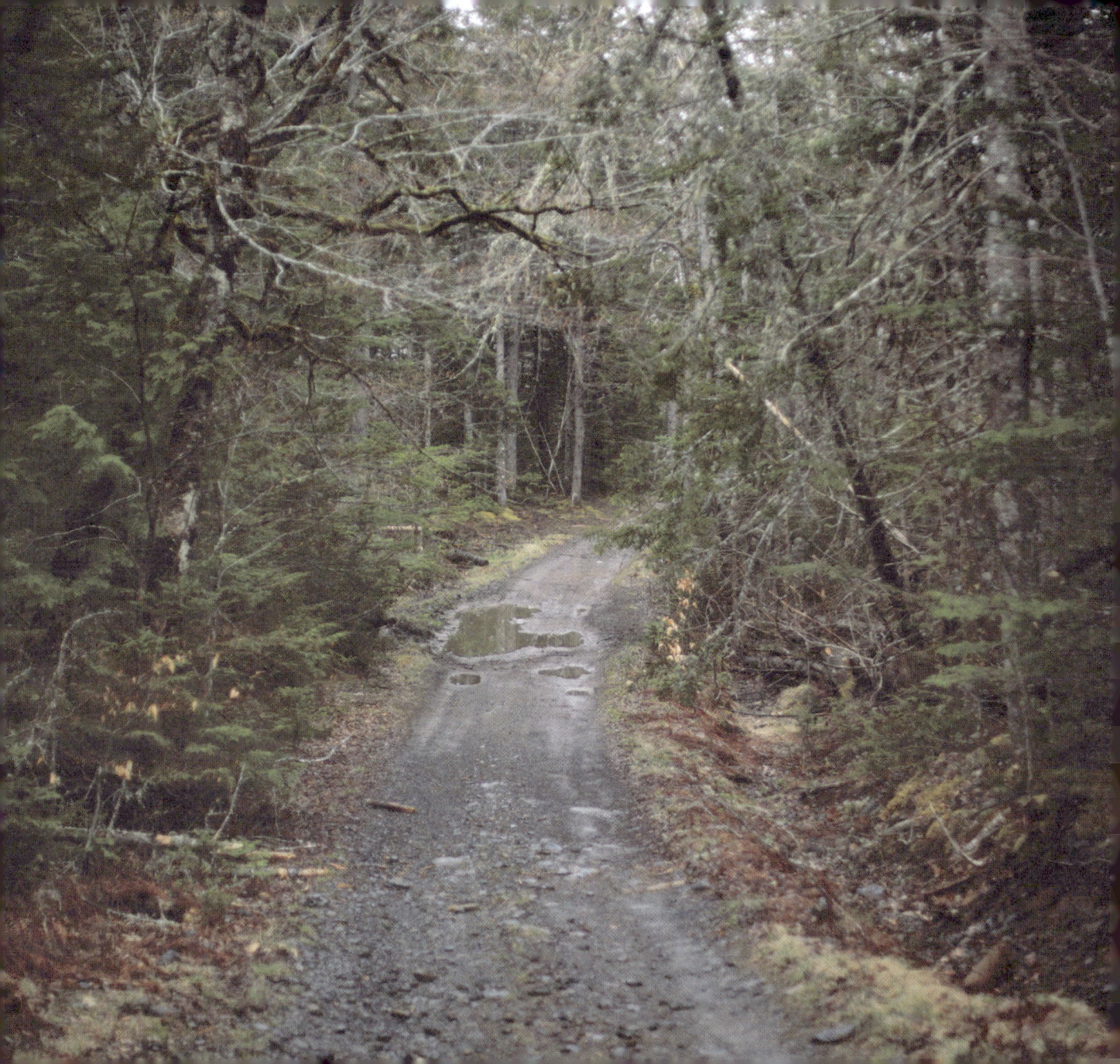

is just about finding where the road goes, following a secret stream or derelict trail, imagining the long-lost lives of abandoned cabins. It's more of an adventure to walk your woods all alone than to follow the hundreds up Mount Everest each year. Just get wandering while you can.

44.97925, -64.21833

5.4 kilometres. Runs northwest from the end of Sangster Bridge Road, crossing Eldridge Road and Allen Brook, ending at Civic #51 on Coach Road, Bishopville. Park at the cul-de-sac. Some variance exists on modern maps, but this is the correct route.

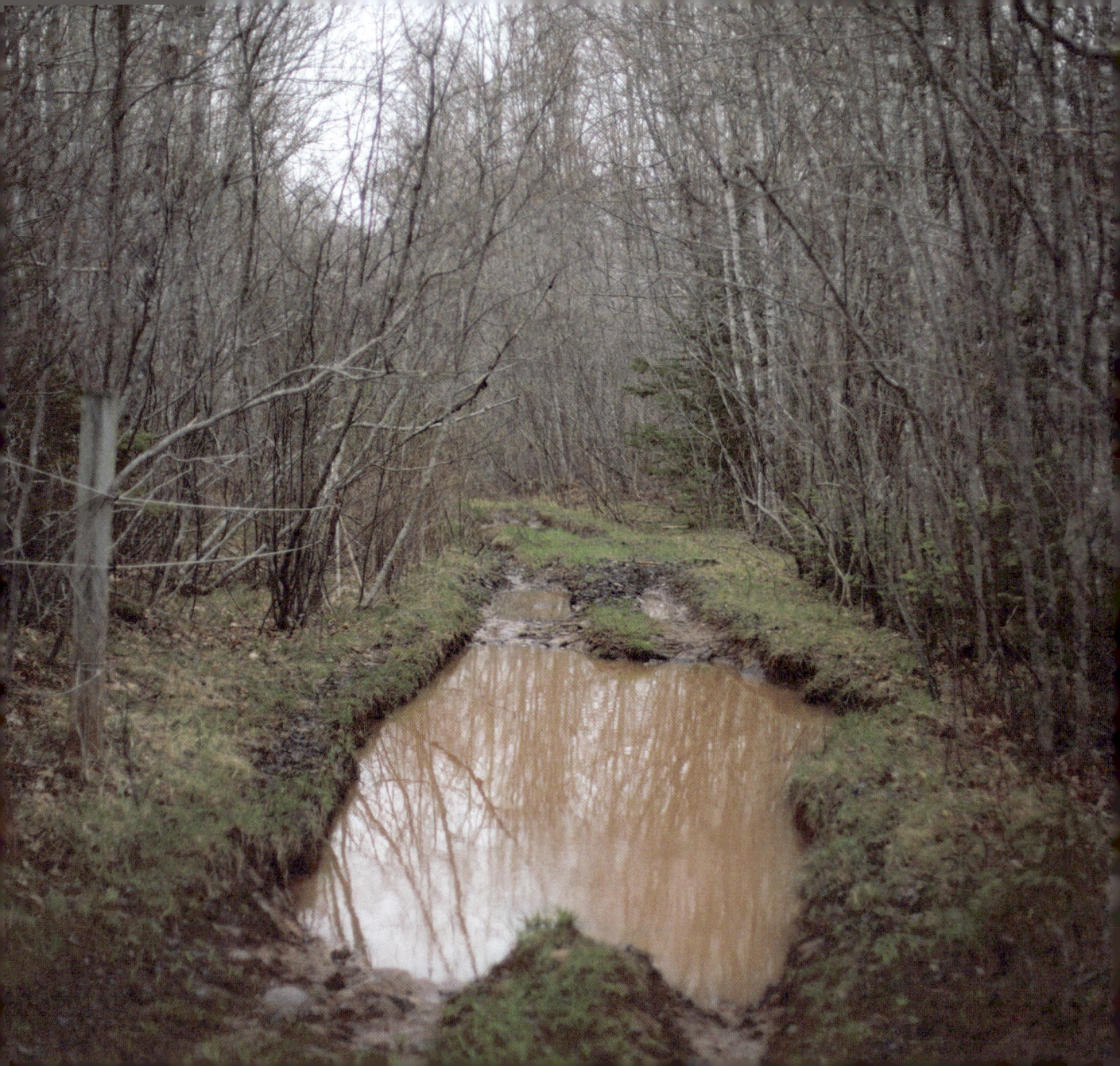

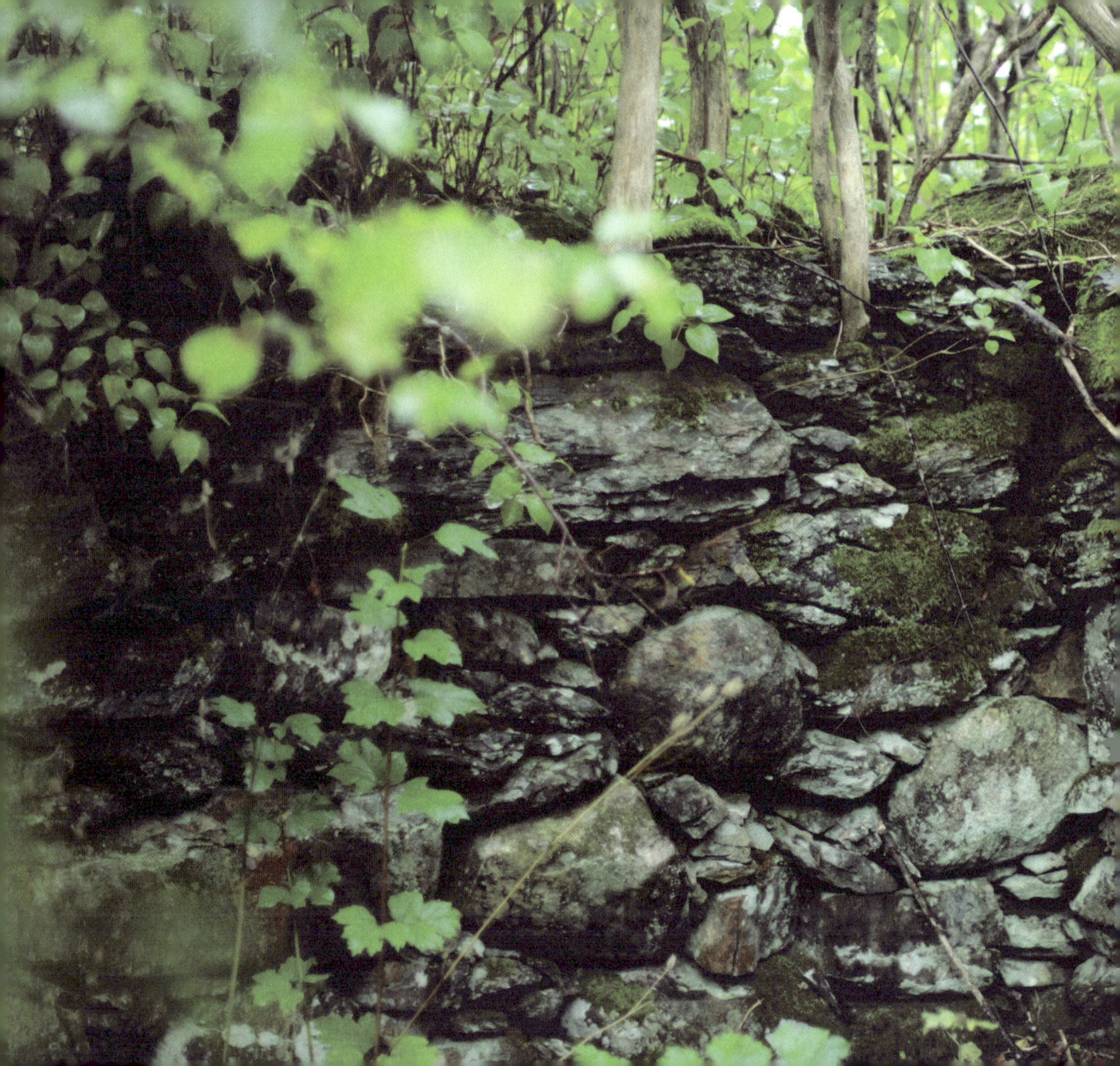

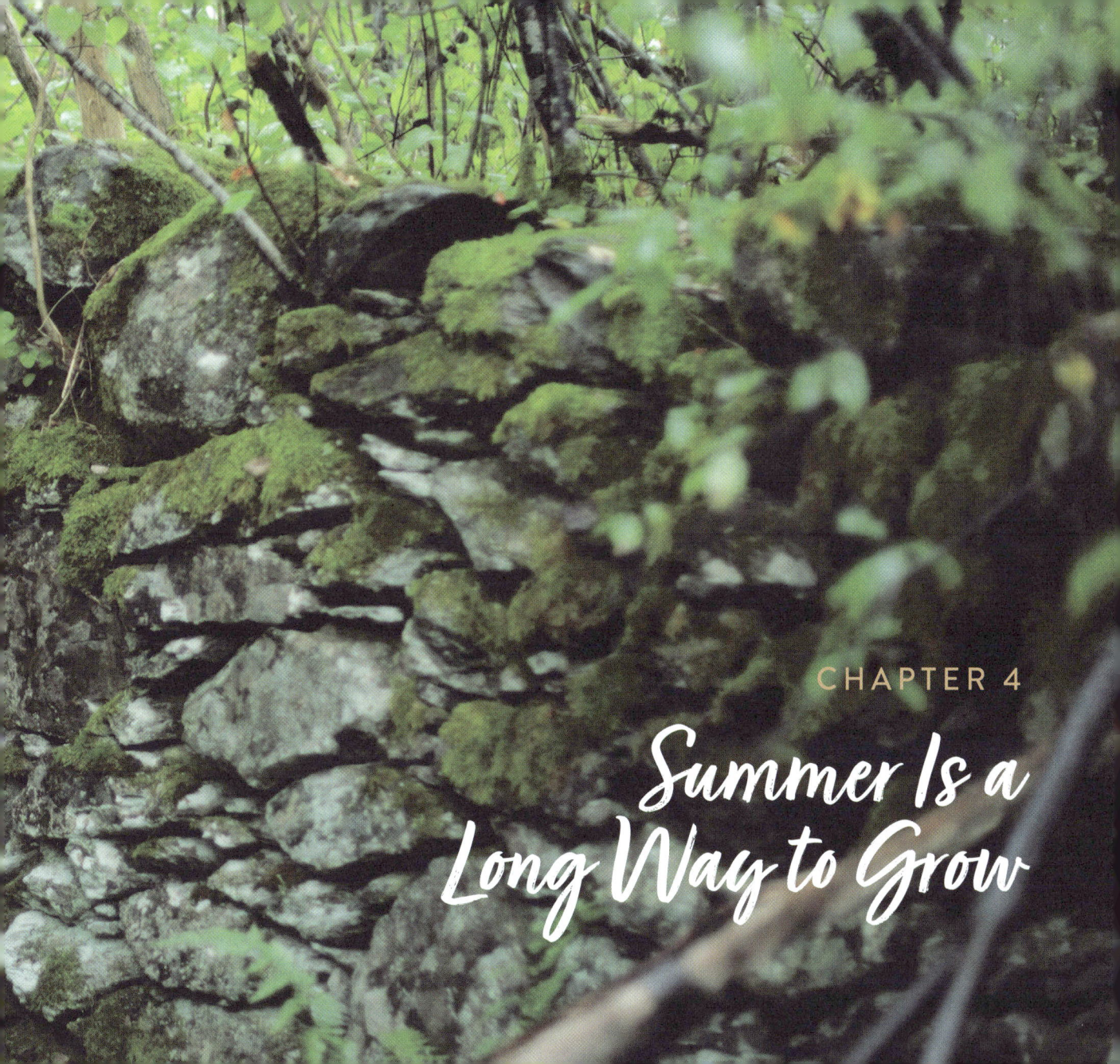

CHAPTER 4

Summer Is a Long Way to Grow

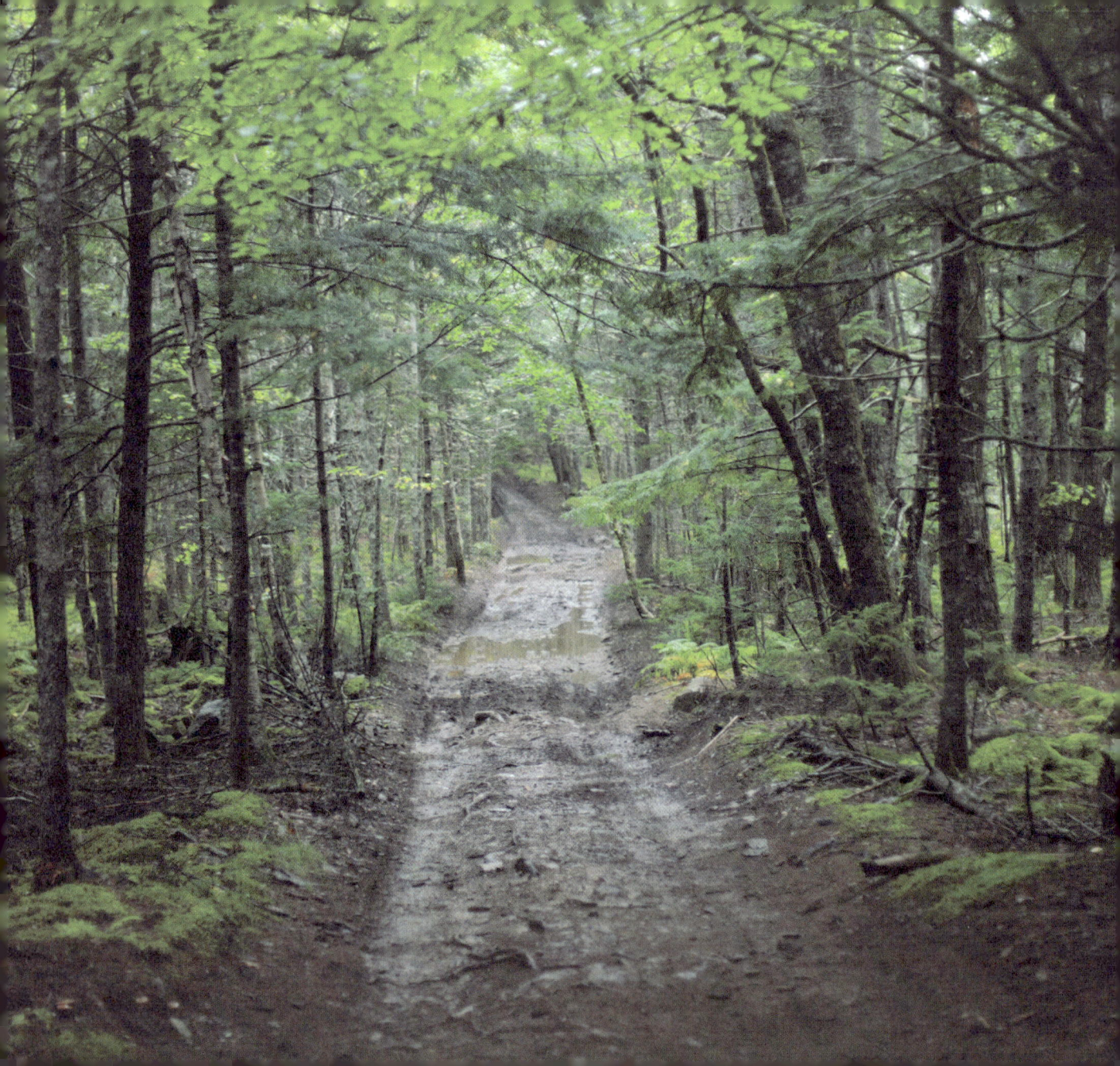

AWALT ROAD

Spectacle Lakes, Lunenburg County

In this place are foundations of stories, untold and true. A couple of centuries back, there were several Dorey families living in these woods. Now, no one at all. In fact, Doreys Lake is the body of water you pass soon after entry, where the cellar of a homestead lingers in a field they cleared. But decades of mispronunciation have truncated it to "Dares Lake" on modern maps. Deeper down is a stream running murky and shallow, spanned by a handmade dam, once holding water for a sawmill site. Out of the dimness of cloud-cast canopy, a thin spot lets light in like a flash, falling on stones set still since before living memory, held with no mortar in place. Beaver Brook had a taste of human retention, when we showed wildlife

what could be done standing upright with opposable thumbs. But our efforts only served a couple of generations, and they've gone on with their satisfied status quo. They only care to conquer one stream at a time, no need to rule the world.

Some places in the forest have a mystery I can barely begin to explain or express. This is the darkest place I've ever been in daylight. Middle of the afternoon, and the pine-shade gloom is so thick it feels like fog. Pupils nearly fully dilated, letting in every ounce of sun; seems like twilight falling with night still hours away. The trees grow taller, and I just keep getting smaller in contrast, until I'm no bigger than I was as a kid. By the end of this road, I'll have shrunk

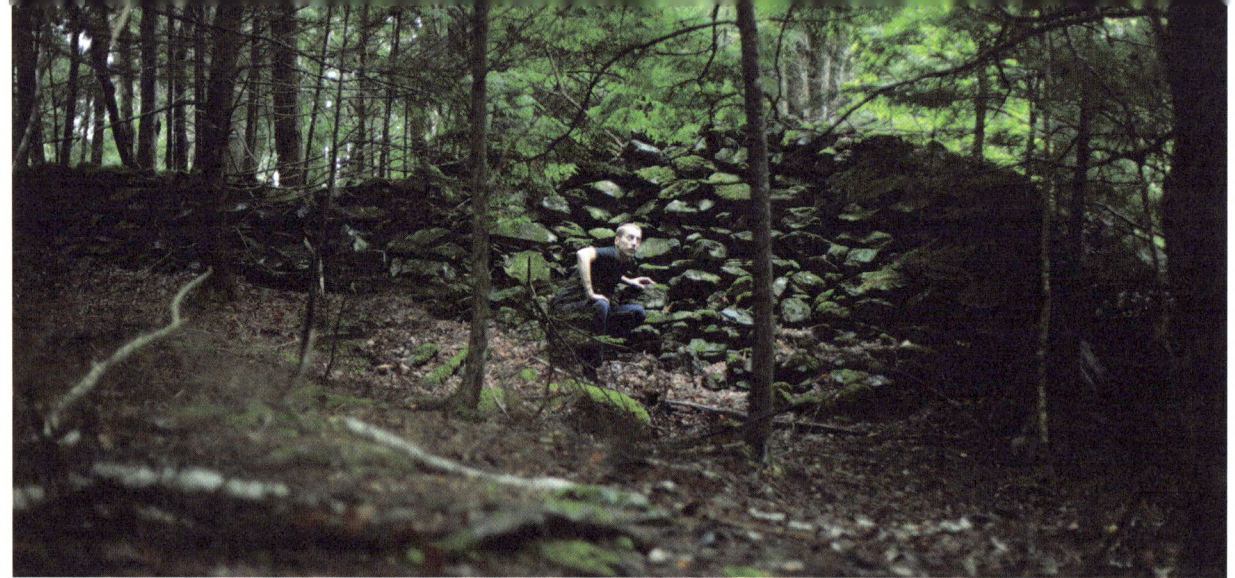

by decades because I can't compete with the age of ancient woods. Awalt Road has a heart that's black but nowhere near empty, signalling signs of life in the vibrating shadows. Some suddenly stirred porcupine crosses paths ahead, birds cry warnings of strangers. There's nothing like the beauty of being where you don't belong for a while. Here, while the dreams run away with me, I'm an intruder.

44.38262, -64.38583

2.5 kilometres. Runs north from Civic #54, passing Dares Lake, up to where regular logging resumes. Park at the paved lot after the last house.

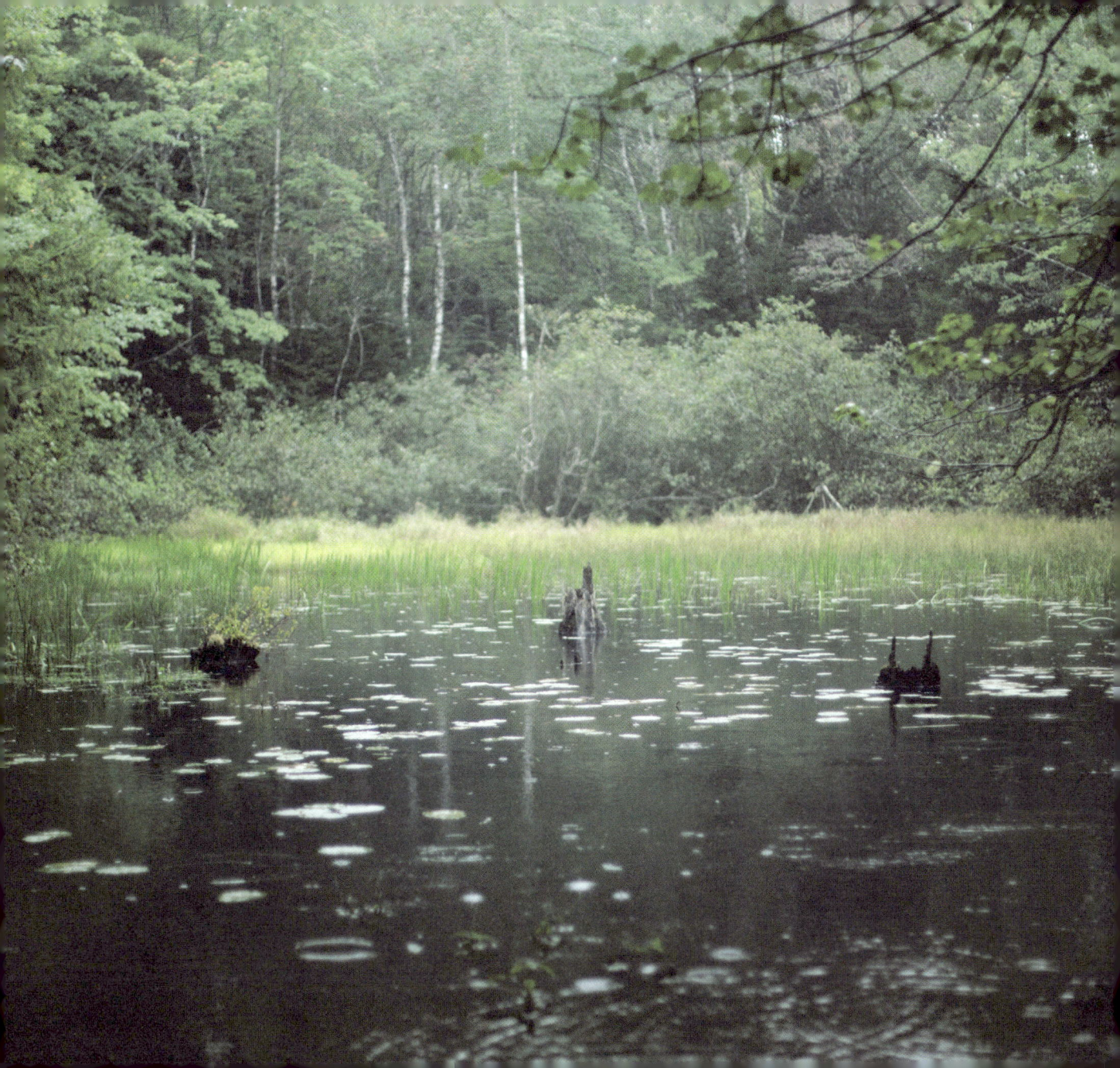

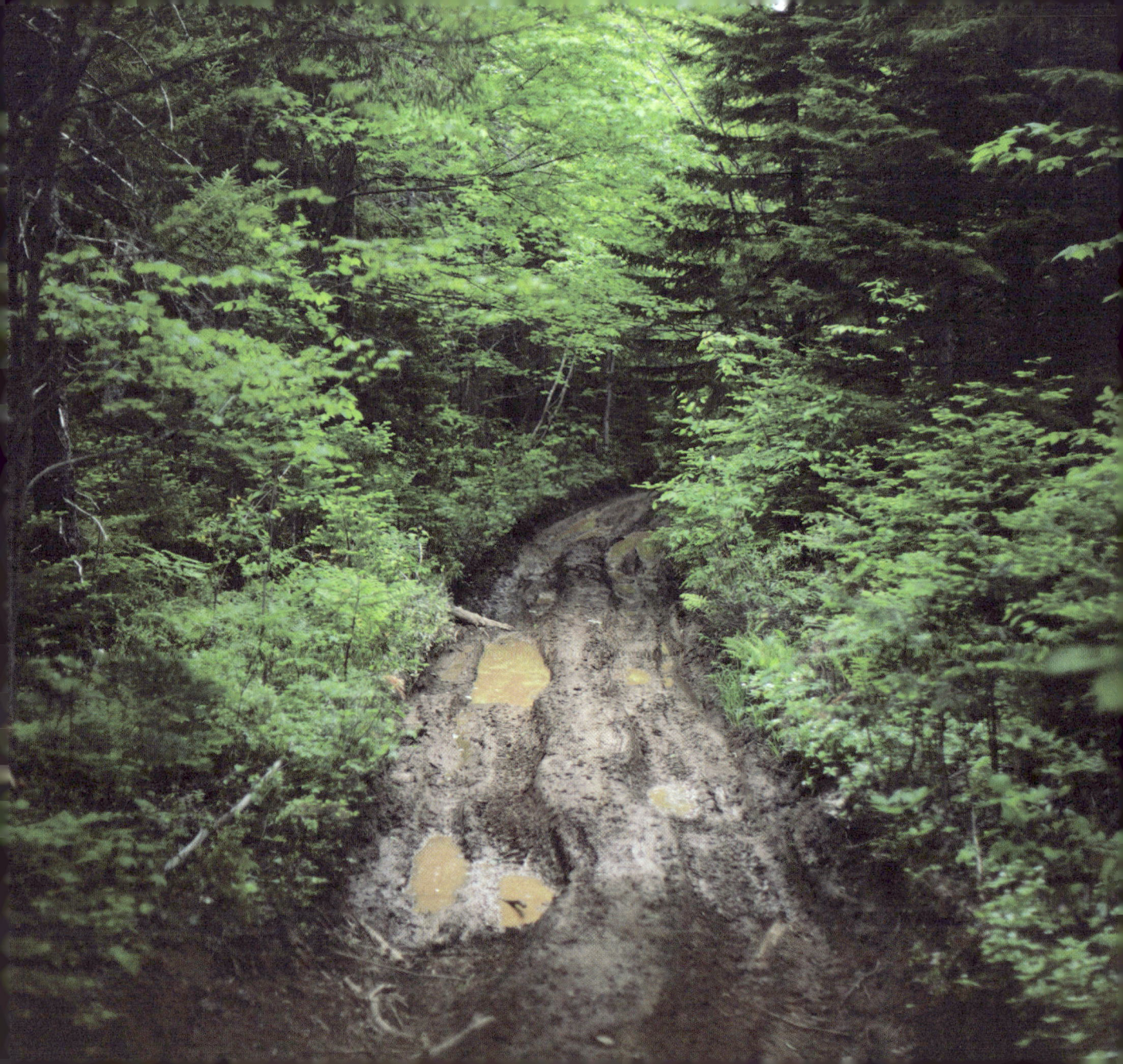

FIELDING ROAD

Robinson Corner, Kings County

The feeling of this forest is like sighing under shelter, a lot of life pushing back against the fears of memory dying. There's thick cloud cover beyond the canopy, and a threat of rain. Leaves diffusing the light and dimming the shadows, I'm inside the green with no hint of the sky. Some kind of down-home adventure here, narrow bends through a sleepy space. Deeper down the road, a couple of turns taken, won't be long before it's woods on all sides. Nature does well in the gloom, signs of life but no map or direction. I slip along a beaver blockade, making a marsh into a tiny lake. Lose count of frogs underfoot, all sorts of trilliums and lady's slippers, more than I've ever seen elsewhere.

But for three long years, Fielding Road was illegally blocked from access. This was the work of a man called Kevin Conrad, and the homemade warning sign was his, everything written on it untrue. It read: "This is not a public road or deeded right of way. It is private." Those are all lies, as Fielding Road is public indeed. It appears as such on every map, including the oldest dating back to 1872, when the Robinson family first settled. More crucially, it's present on the current Department of Public Works records as K-Class, an unmaintained public road. Property records agree, as well.

For a few hundred metres, where this public right of way borders his property, Mr. Conrad felled dozens of trees across the path. He parked his RV there, and his excavator, which he'd been using to clear an area for construction. But what happened on this

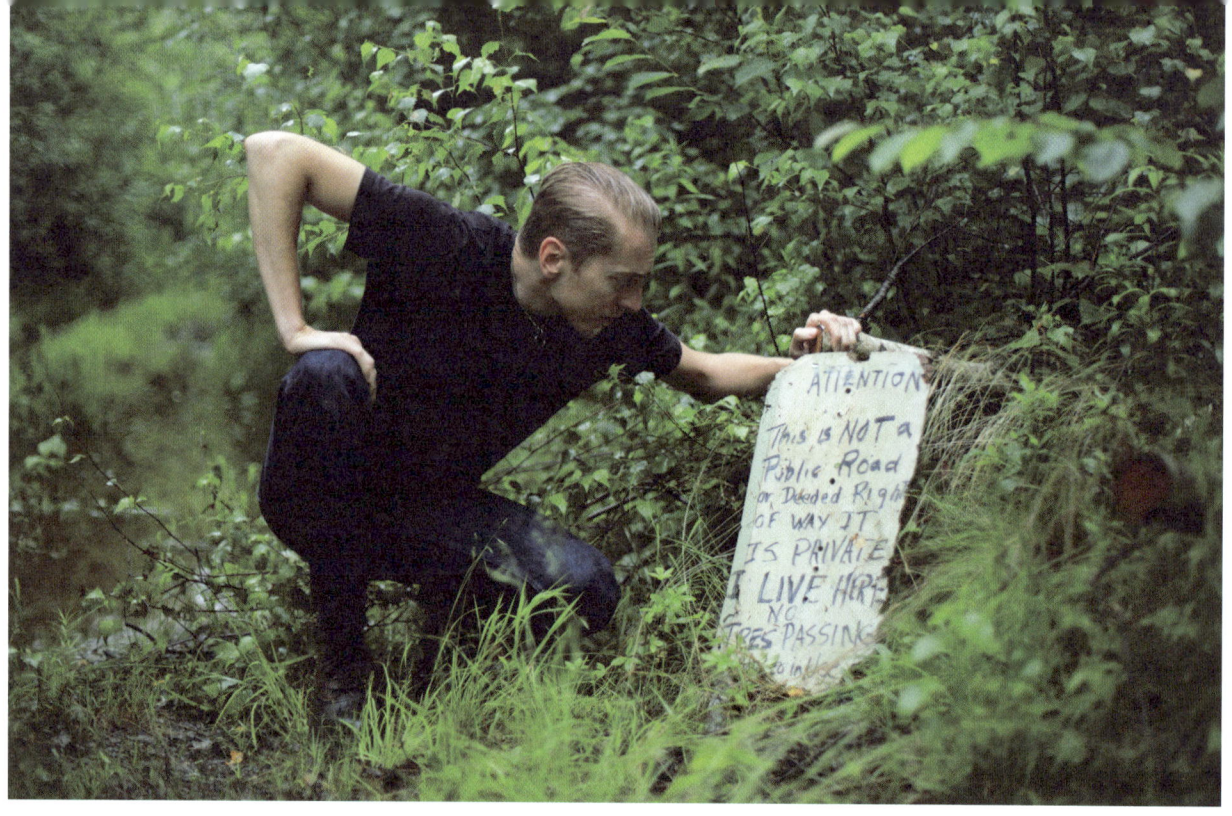

bit of land two decades earlier is far more worrying. November 2006 marked the discovery of the body of Leslie Ann Conrad, found by a hunter in a shallow grave. She was Kevin's wife, gone missing since October, a fact he hadn't bothered to report himself. The police investigated him but never filed charges. Ever since that event, he had been the prime suspect in her murder—but remained free due to lack of evidence.

I passed by here in the dying days of April, and noticing no one around, pulled up at the corner and walked the first kilometre—ducking under and climbing over felled trunks. On my way back, I tore down all misleading warning signs. After heading

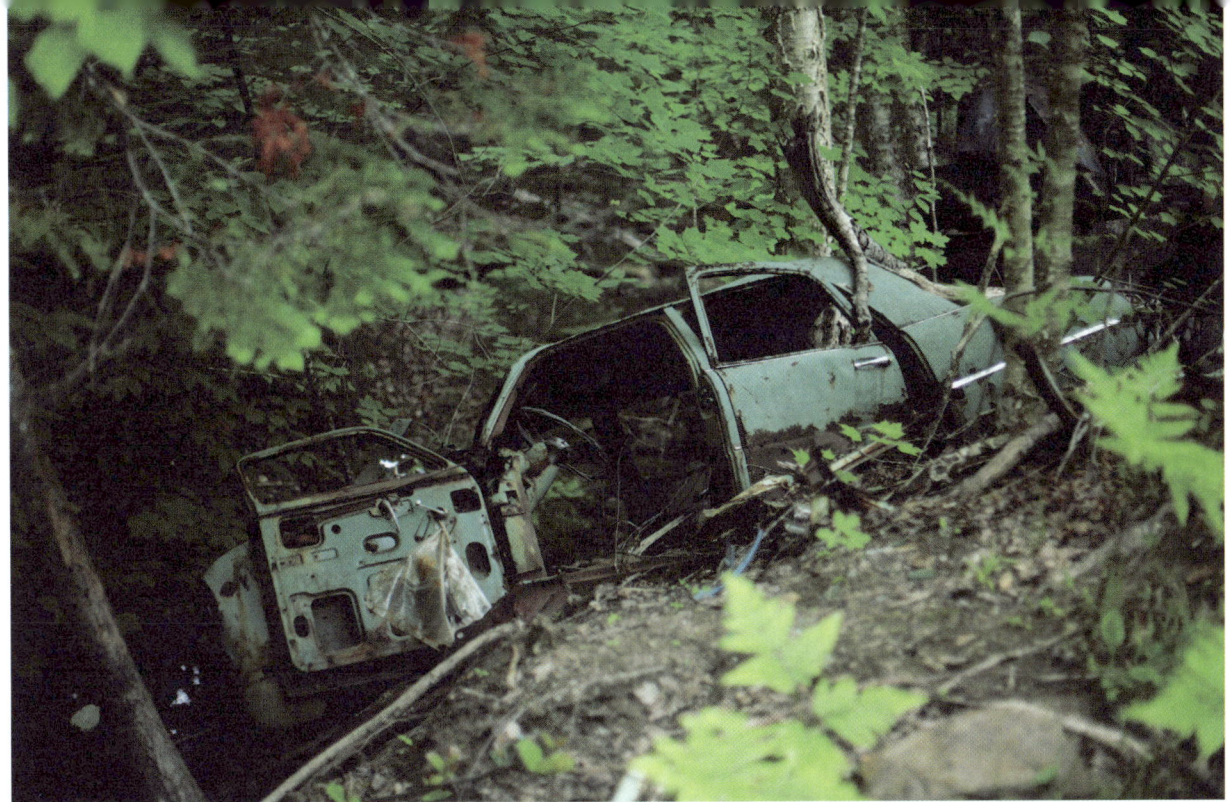

home, this road never crossed my mind through the following months. But then I stumbled on a news story saying that Kevin Conrad was discovered dead in his excavator on May 1, just four days after my last visit. He might well have been in there when I passed by. I remember spotting his machine through the trees, mired in the mud, and it hadn't moved from that position in the newspaper photos. His death was ruled to be of natural causes.

What does all this mean? Well, for wanderers like me, there's no one stopping us from using Fielding Road. But for the children of Leslie Ann Conrad, the man they suspect of murdering their mother will never be held accountable. Perhaps there's a certain

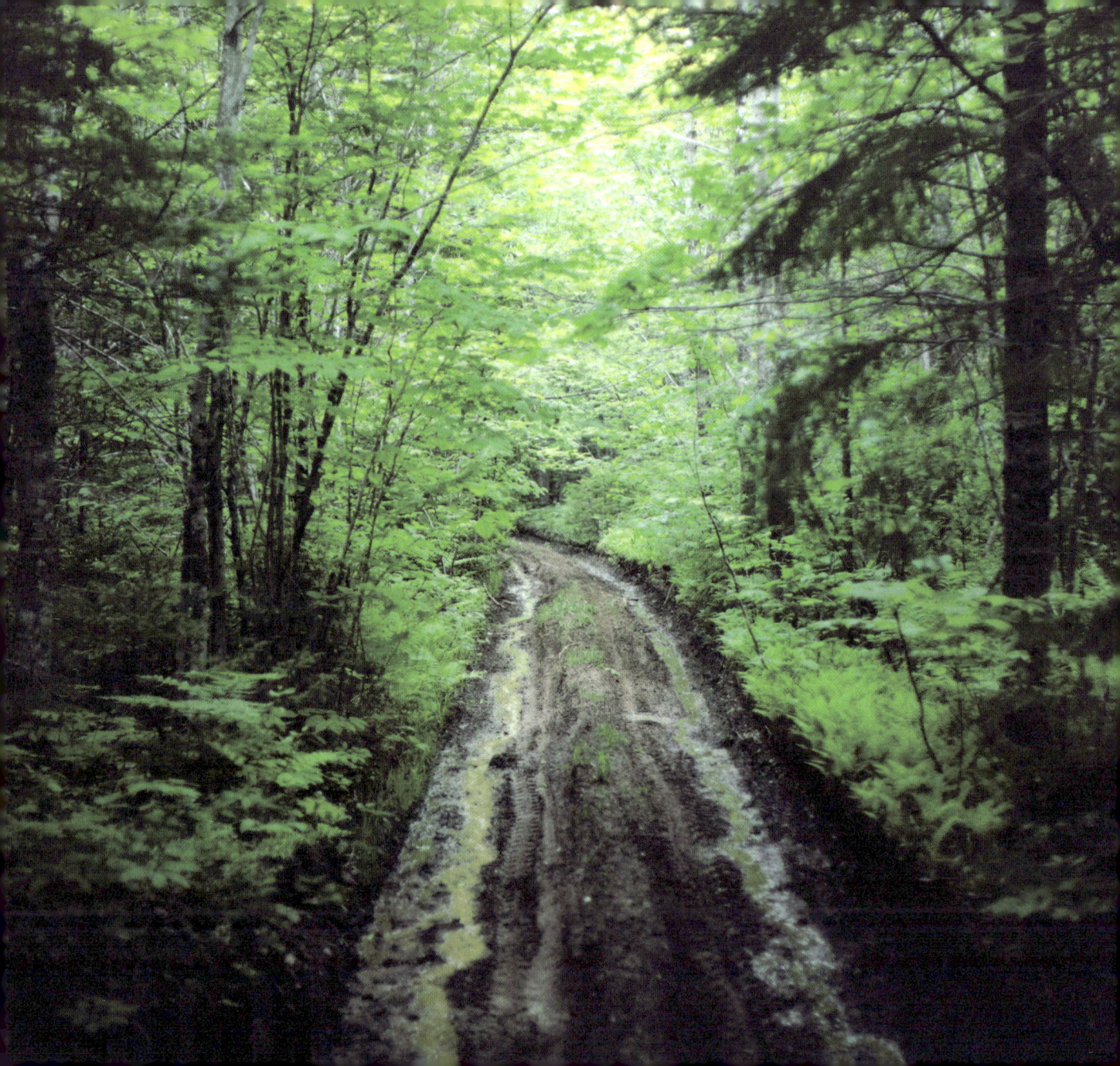

closure in knowing that he's gone from the land of the living, closure and an opening. The death of a lie about what was and wasn't, and some sort of path to the future.

The woman who was buried here was an active hiker herself. Leslie Ann Conrad represented Nova Scotia at the 1978 National Campers and Hikers Association Campvention in Colorado. I imagine she'd have hated to see a heartwaking trail like this restricted from public access. She was loved, cared for, and remembered. Like most tragic tales, all is not resolved—but some, in the end, is restored.

45.04854, -64.29142

4.6 kilometres. Runs east from the corner of Melanson Road and Peck Meadow Road, coming out near Civic #542 in Lockhartville. Park at the corner.

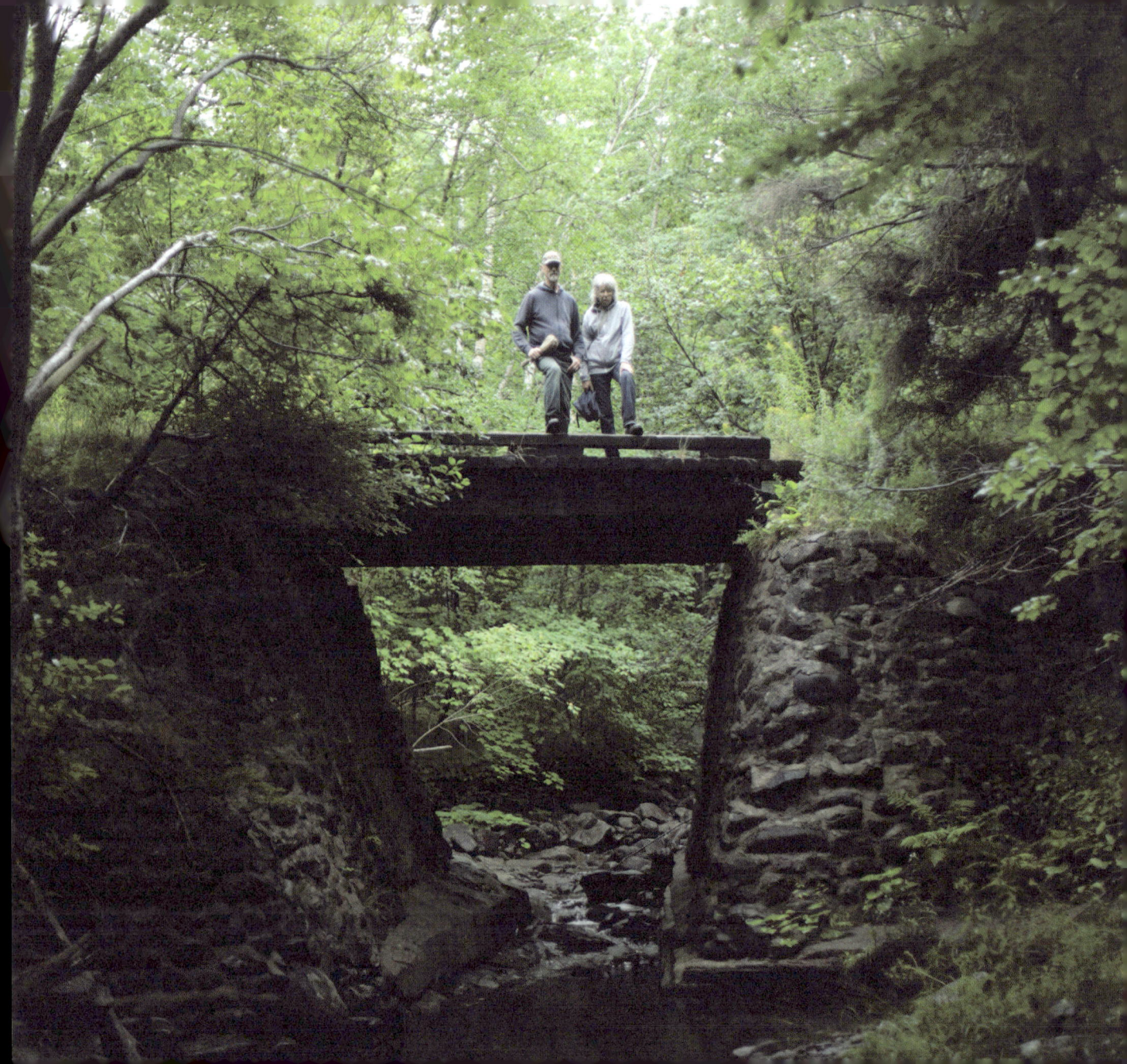

BROAD COVE ROAD

Bay View, Digby County

Here on the road west from Point Prim there are many remnants of homesteads, built by the families Adams, Middleton, Stark, and Sweeney. Very little lingers of them now, dirt cellars dug below structures long gone. Carefully stacked walls have been reduced to craters, softened by a century of spreading roots and erosion. Proud story of the effort it took to make a living on hard earth. Along this three-kilometre stretch of derelict road, it's no wonder no one remains. Finding foundations can be an exhausting experience, but every time I stumble over one, it's like uncovering an open grave. In terms of memories, they're no less tied to life.

Proceed at Own Risk. You'll never see a set of warning signs like these that don't mean it. Someone told me about their ill-advised adventure attempting to drive Broad Cove Road in a regular car. Even if you make it through intact, you'll likely bottom out a few times. If you've got a vehicle with the clearance to miss that, still expect a good set of scratches up your side doors for the effort. I've made that mistake myself all over these woods, done my fair share of fifteen-minute backups and twelve-point turnarounds. But usually I remember to just pull up and step out, give my back a break from sitting too long, and get walking. Off-roading is the other option, but I can't

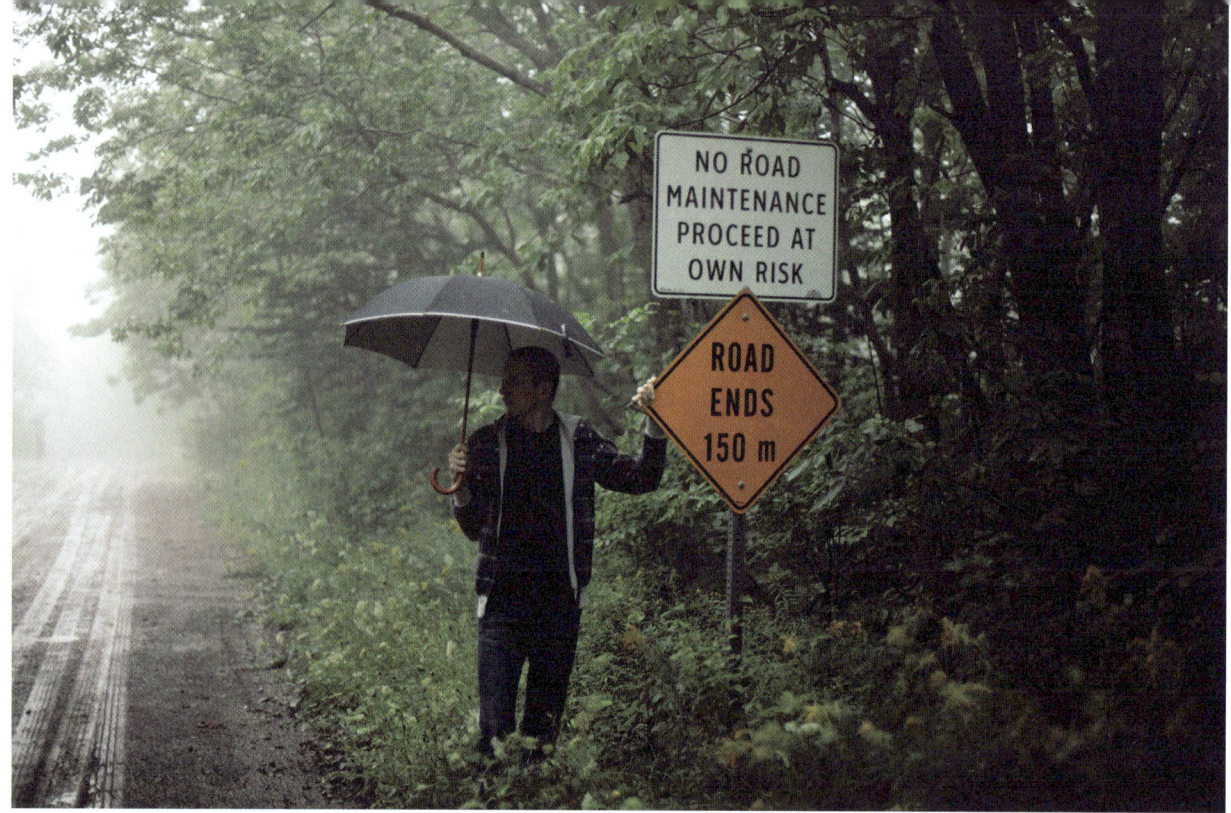

be bothered to buy and haul a second set of wheels around. Seems wrong anyhow to fill the forest with some noisy reason to keep me out of shape. My legs still have what it takes to keep me going. I'll push them till they fail me.

I'm in a mist so thick I can feel it on my skin; clouds come to earth and enveloping. Now the trees draw in, and I see secrets around every corner. There's nothing big about them, just the sort of pull that always lies in not knowing what's next. On this old way along the coast from Bay View to Culloden, down an abandoned road no longer needed, it's a while through the woods to get there. There's a magic called "closeness" that I can be tricked into believing, a sleight of heart and,

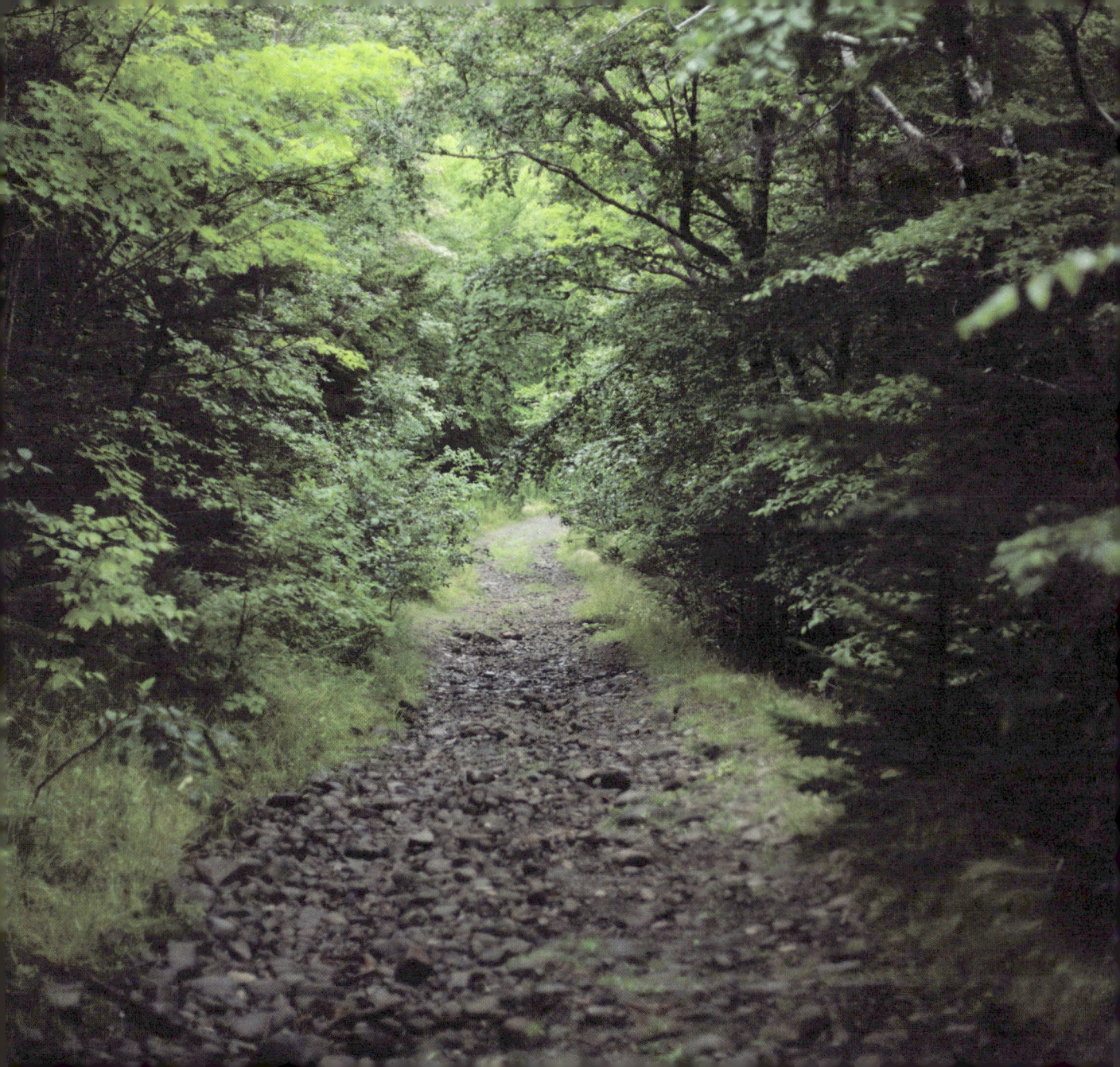

sure enough, we'll arrive eventually. After a lot of stony stumbling, there's a tall, narrow bridge near the end, spanning Micmac Brook. It's like much of the road on the way—high and dry from low surroundings, somehow looking down on things. I've always been a little alone in my thinking, tending towards an outside mindset. But I'm right in the middle in the derelict forest, walking where every wild thing is living, on a road that splits the centre.

44.68193, -65.78502

3.4 kilometres. Runs west past the former quarry and over Micmac Brook to Culloden Road. Park at the wide spot 150 metres west of Civic #2481.

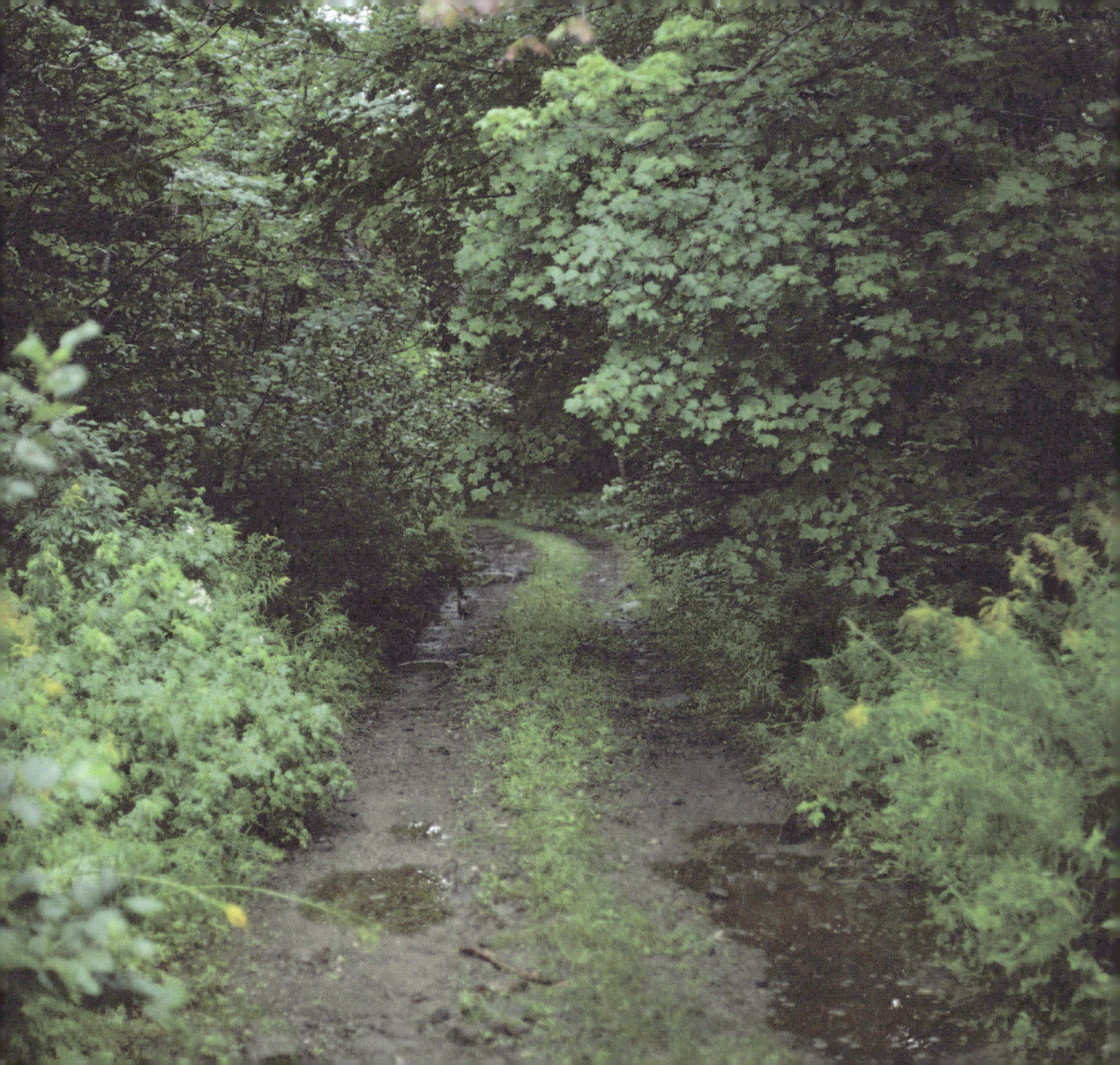

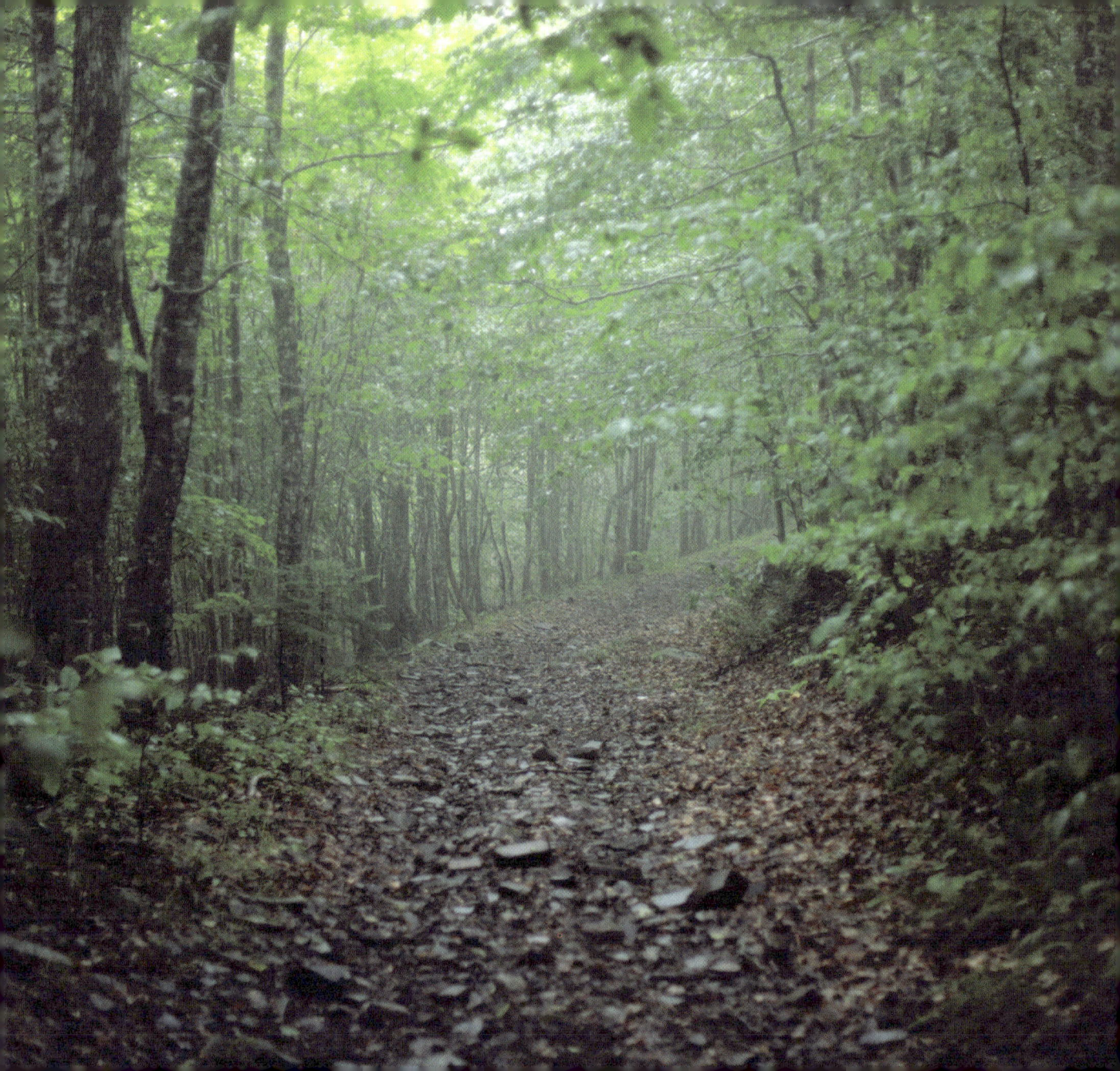

WITHERS MOUNTAIN ROAD

Granville Centre, Annapolis County

Hiking in the pouring rain never gets old for me. It has a way of recreating each familiar sight, making me feel like these well-worn ruts cut trails I've never trodden. True enough, this is only the sixth time I've made the long, hard climb all the way up from the Valley floor. But spread out through the years, I've learned the bends and curves and tallest trees like friends you might keep honestly. Or, at least, friendly strangers waved down in passing. Unlike many other twisting switchbacks in these parts, this one was never known as a hub of humanity. Trees to harvest and a way over North Mountain were the main intended purposes. The oldest mention I can find is on a map from 1876, when this path was

called "Weather's Road," and the tiny body of water it reached was "Clements Lake." Some time since, the names were changed to "Withers Mountain Road" and "Eaton Lake," but the woods are still as silent as way back when.

Far as I know, not a single year-round settlement was ever raised through here. A handful of cabins exist today — the newest one built in just the past couple of years, and others more rustic, dating back to previous decades. I sort of waved hello to each today, but as usual, no one was home. Just at the foothills, a derelict logging truck sits rusting in a clearing, slowly consumed by brush. Under the canopy, a towering tree stands at the start of the steepest

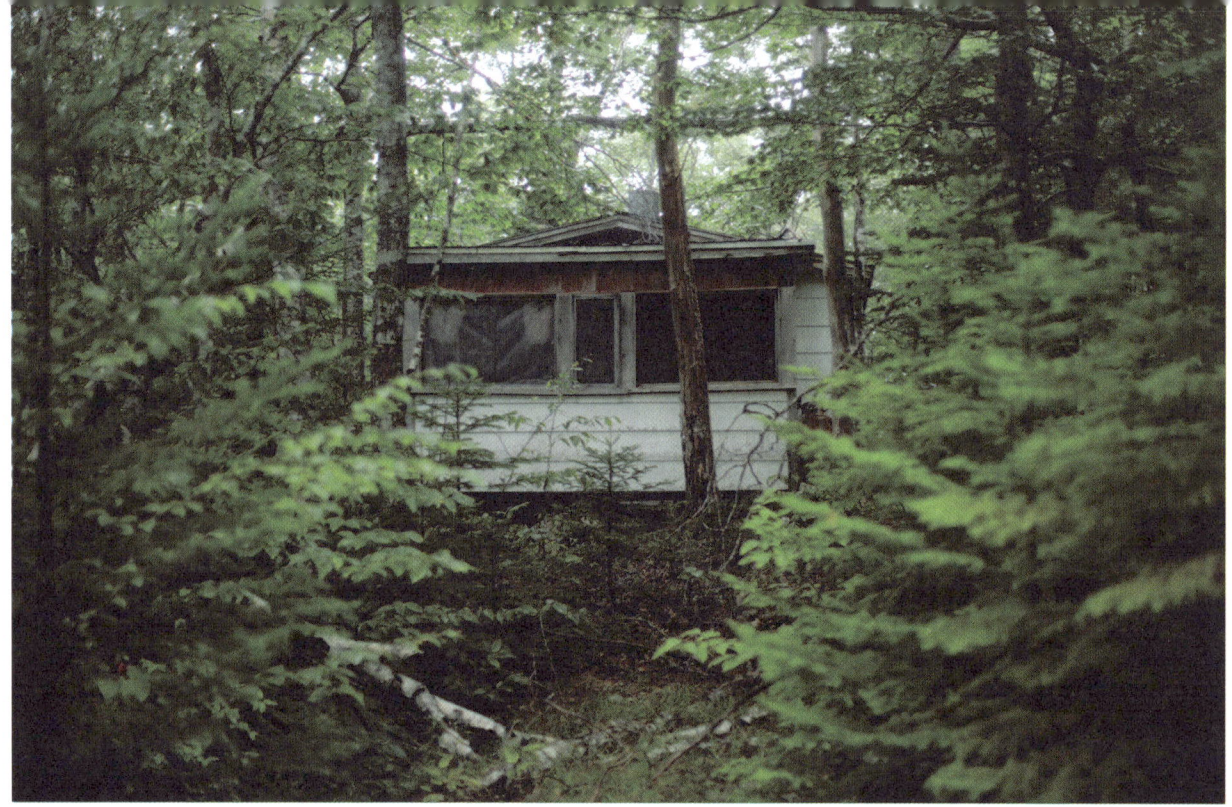

section, competing for the height it could've claimed if only it set root elsewhere. Every time someone says I'm tall, I think of places like this. In context of the forest, I never feel anything but impossibly short. I suspect that there will come this way the old, unshakable urge again. You know it well—the clear-cutter's drive to bring it all down. When I'm out somewhere somewhat wondrous, all I can hope is against it happening.

I never know for sure how it'll go on a long mountain climb, but I always hope to have my head in the clouds. I've had a lot of dark days lately—sunny ones, specifically—so I've been craving the escape of a world a little more restrained. Vanishing points and

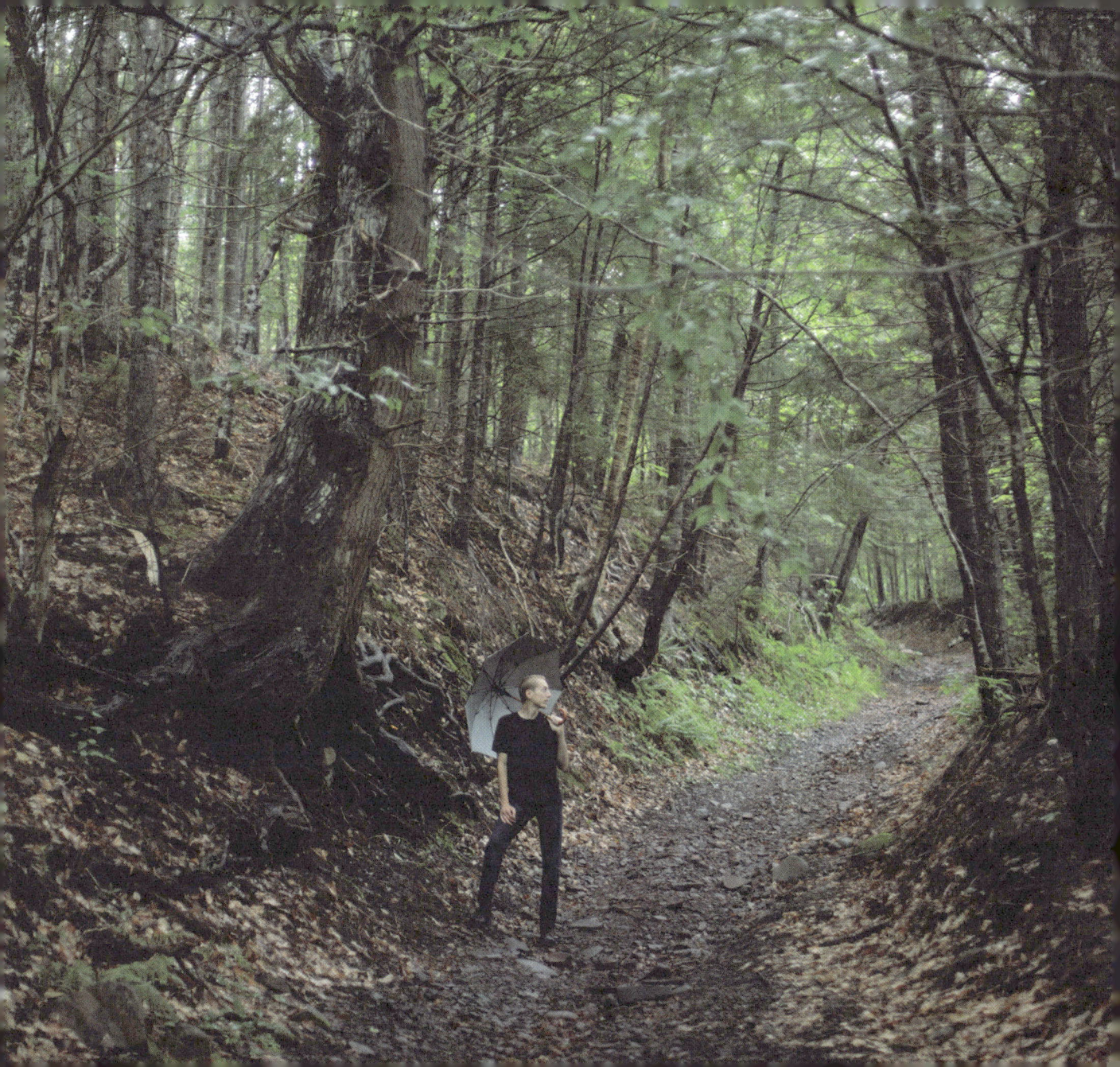

trees on all sides, just take away the future and give me a whole lot more inescapable present. I've found sometimes that I can't think about less unless possibilities are limited. In the wet and tangled woods, there is only one direction or decision. I'm going straight to where the road runs out, then I'm going back where I came from. All the rain-soaked leaves make decisions for me. Since I'm disinclined to hike home drenched head to toe, I'll stick to the relative dryness underfoot. The colour in everything is coming truer. The shimmer of wet light off rocks, and the mist that takes away what's next—everything about a rainy day makes my method of being alive a little easier.

44.77118, -65.46740

3.6 kilometres. Runs north from Civic #5416 on Highway 1, up North Mountain to Eaton Lake. Don't block the road; park 270 metres west at All Saints Anglican graveyard.

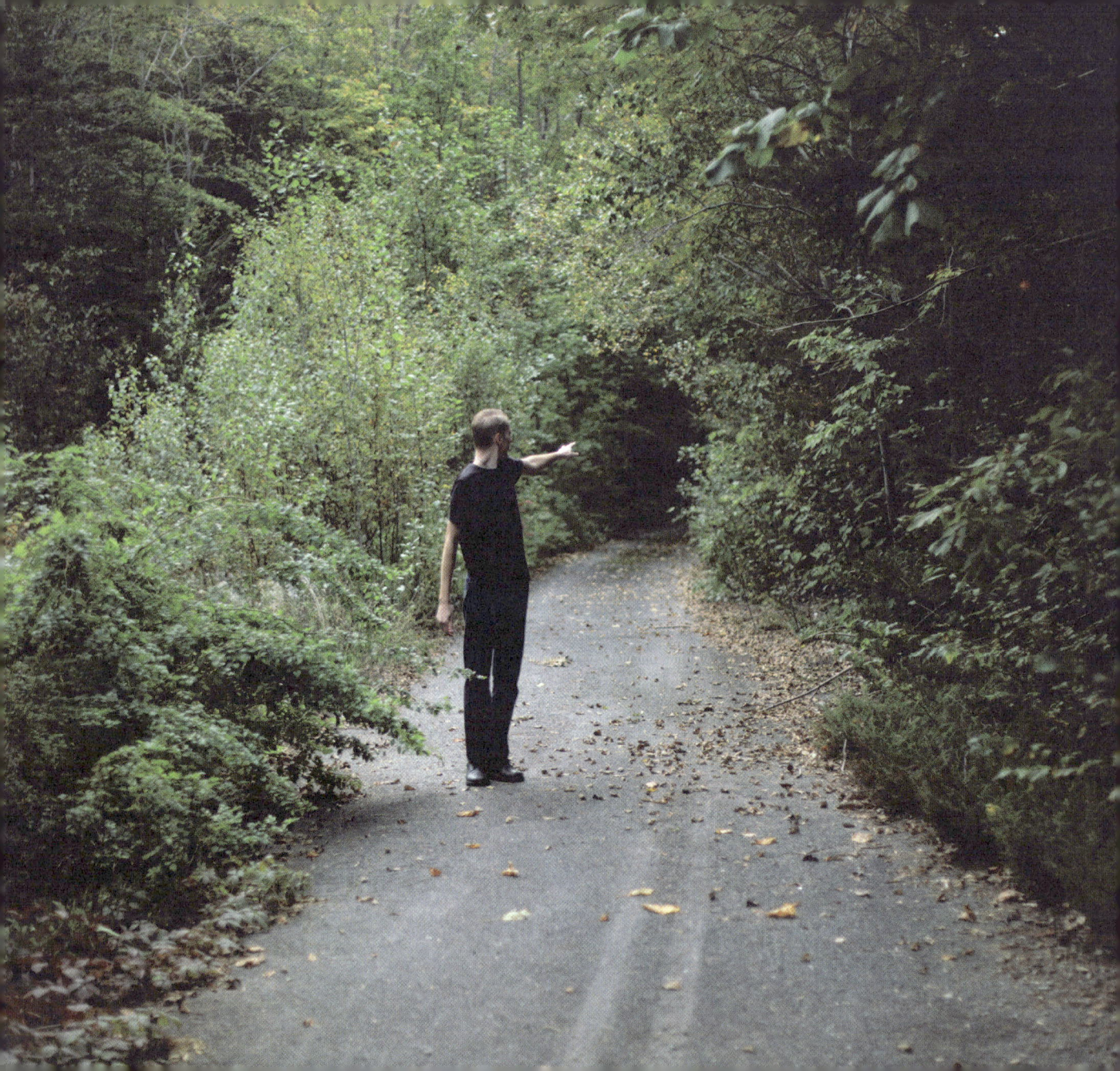

CANAAN MOUNTAIN ROAD

Canaan, Kings County

Muddy abandoned roads are common sights, but to find one paved is rare indeed. I've loved this short, mysterious span for quite some time, the old way off South Mountain before Highway 101 cut it in two. This was once meant to be co-opted for the main exit to New Minas, but when it got rerouted a little farther east, this was left as a dead end ever after. Dotted lines still show in faded aspect, and the trees and moss attempt to narrow its borders. A few years back, some troublemaking locals attempted to claim it as their own, father and son felling trees and blocking access. It was a real mess that they had no right to make, but others came to clear it away—offering a reminder that this public road is, in fact, public. They've seemed shy to break the law ever since.

This limbo between habitation and dereliction is a world that's somehow made for me. I get into it easily and feel more alive when I've made my way out. Swaying leaves and the trickle of some unnamed brook—it's nearly enough to drown the highway traffic and carry silence home. Right at the borders, trees try and fail to take over, settling for available sun like a skylight overhead. Now I'm walking in the arbor, just a tiny thing so far as the woods are concerned. A few years back,

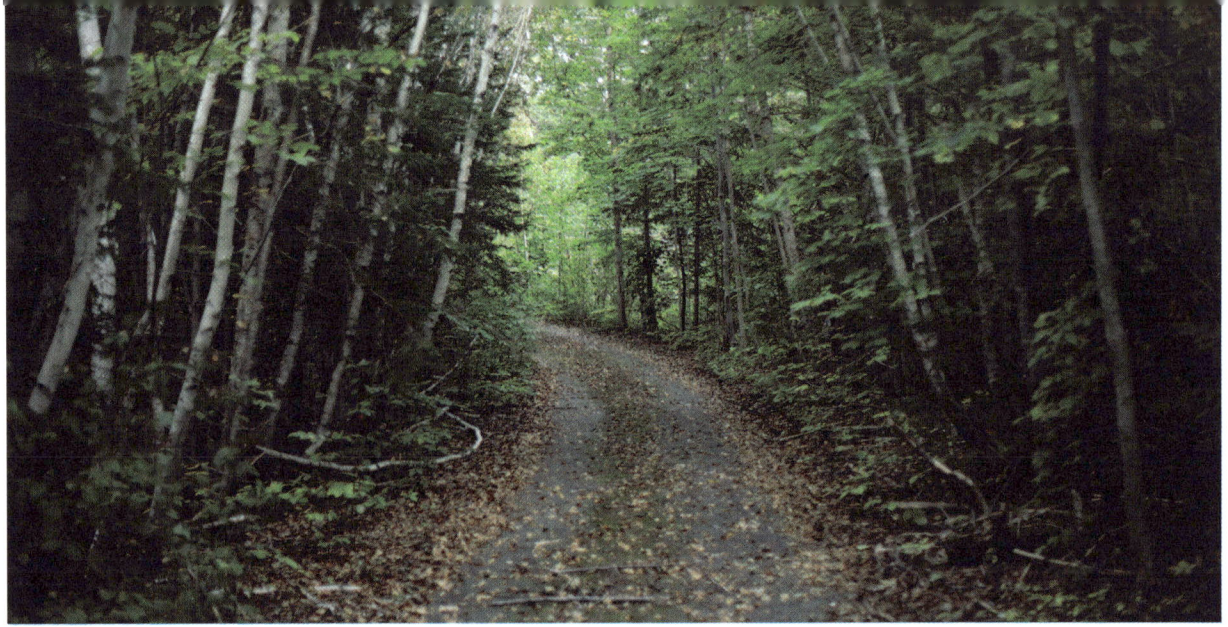

I took Julianne Hazlewood from CBC Radio on a walk through here, and while she recorded what I perceived to be silence, I realized what sound had to offer. Dancing branches, footsteps falling, cars in the distance, a dog barking. All my little senses making sense of natural chaos. Do I hear me now?

45.04882, -64.48593

450 metres. Runs north from just after Civic #1160 down to Highway 101. Park on the shoulder.